Corporate Guru

Dhirubhai Ambani

Prateeksha M. Tiwari

DIAMOND BOOKS

ISBN : 978-81-288-2428-9
© Publisher

Published by
Diamond Pocket Books (P) Ltd.
X-30, Okhla Industrial Area, Phase - II
New Delhi - 110 020
Phone : 011-41611861, 40712100
Fax : 011-41611866
E-mail : sales@dpb.in
Website : www.dpb.in

Edition : 2010

Printed at
Adarsh Printers, Shahdara, Delhi-110032

Corporate Guru: Dhirubhai Ambani
by: *Prateeksha M. Tiwari*

Introduction

What do you call a man who hated to lose?... A winner?... That is too easy, too glib, and buries the story. All Dhirajlal Hirachand Ambani (Dhirubhai) ever wanted to be the biggest there ever is, the best there ever was. He wanted a piece of the action—preferably all of it. If others weren't let him in, he created his own turf and own it all.

Dhirubhai was actually a businessman, but his career was so extraordinary that he was more than just a businessman, more than even an industrialist. He was a folk hero to millions of Indians, even those who were not businessmen, or does not aspire for a business career. Without Dhirubhai, we would not have learnt how to think big, not in terms of a small factory here and there, but in terms of giant plants, as big as anywhere in the world and as modern as they come. Dhirubhai taught

India to think big and he usually said. *"Ours is a big country and if we do not think big, we shall never be able to attain our potential."*

It is not easy to think big in India. We are so worried about the next meal that there is no time for anything else. For the last thousand years we have not thought big at all. We can think only of the next meal, the next pay cheque, the next job, the next election. We can never think of the day after tomorrow, let alone the year after tomorrow, or the generation after the next. We are so poor that everything tends to be short-term, small and trifling, and almost always temporary and short-lived.·

How did Dhirubhai learn to think big?...He was a son of a village teacher in a small place in Gujarat and was sent to Mumbai as a boy of fifteen or so, as there were no jobs for him in his village. He was then packed off to Aden, where he worked as a petrol pump attendant. Later, he went on to East Africa where he also worked in an oil company, also as an assistant before he returned to India for good.

When he returned to Mumbai, he started his own yarn dealership, in a small 10 x 10 room in Mulji Jetha market, for which he paid an exorbitant rent (at that time) of 150 rupees a month, just because it had a telephone.

As a yarn merchant, he used to go from one dealer to another and also to purchase agents of the big textile companies in Mumbai, most of whom have now shut up shop or gone bankrupt. Ambani remembered them and called them his *seths*. But how was it that Dhirubhai went on to chemicals from textiles, and from there to petrochemicals and then to oil exploration?

Dhirubhai was thinking big even when he was small. His company, Reliance Industries, went public in 1977, when the turnover was around Rs. 100 crore, not a great deal of money even 25 years ago. He was still a small man, though he was being watched carefully by people in Mumbai. But he was thinking not of his 100-crore business, not how to make it to 200 crore, but how to take his company to the top. He was not only thinking big, he had solid plans to go big. He had projections for his own company, Reliance. For Dhirubhai, textiles was only a beginning of his dreams. He had worked out in his mindscape what he would do five, ten, fifteen years after, and he had formed a complete strategy for doing what he wanted to do.

Dhirubhai was never a big talker. But after a good lunch and some dessert, he relaxed in his office, and talked about this and that, until it was time for him to go back to work. He was then still in textiles and did not have a single chemical plant. He had thorough knowledge about the synthetics industry and all those chemicals with fancy names which only a qualified chemicals engineer would know. For such an exceptional knowledge he said, *"I meet lots of people and read lots of literature. And I know exactly how to go from this to that point, and do what I want to do."*

Dhirubhai rarely talked about money, though that was supposed to be his forte. He was known in the market as a financial wizard. He raised Rs. 7,500 crore in all for his business, huge amount even for a man like Dhirubhai.

Dhirubhai started at the bottom with a small weaving mill and ended up with an oil refinery. When he died Dhirubhai was known as a petroleum man, not a textile man, because textiles accounted for only 2 per cent of his total turnover of over Rs. 60,000 crores.

Where did Dhirubhai learn to think big?...He did not learn anything from his business contemporaries because there was nothing to learn. He was born thinking big. It was second nature to him, otherwise how could a man in a dingy office hawking yarn ended up as the owner of a huge petrochemical plant and an equally huge oil refinery?

He was a restless soul who simply had to do what he did, because that was his compulsion. Everything else came afterwards, as it does when you know what you are going to do, though not how you are going to do it.

If the first half of the 20th century belonged to Tatas, the second half belonged to Dhirubhai Ambani.

-Prateeksha M. Tiwari

The Ambani Family Tree

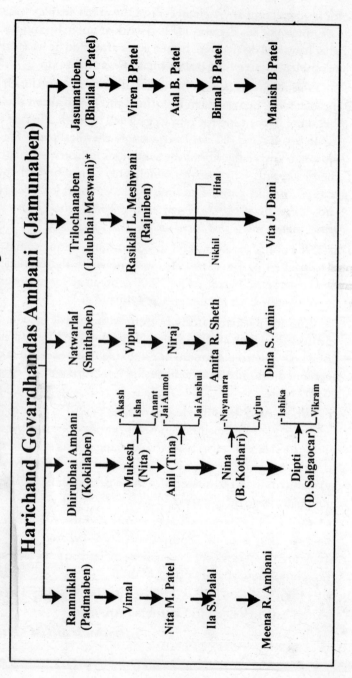

Contents

Honours & Accolades

Inherited Rich Legacy

Personal Details in Nutshell

INTRODUCING
A BUSINESS TYCOON

Dhirubhai Ambani

Dhirajlal Hirachand Ambani was born on 28 December 1932, at Chorwad, Junagadh in the state of Gujarat, India, into a Modh family of very moderate means. He was the third son of a school teacher. When he was 16 years old, he moved to Aden, Yemen. Initially Dhirubahi worked as a despatch clerk with A. *Besse & Co*. Two years later, *A. Besse & Co*. became distributor for *Shell products* and Dhirubhai was promoted to manage the company's oil-filling station at the port of Aden. He was married to Kokilaben and had two sons and two daughters.

In the 1950s the *Yemini* administration realized that their main unit of currency *Rial* was in disappearing. After investigating the matter it was realized that all Rials were routed to the Port City of Aden. There a young man in twenties was placing unlimited *buy orders* of Yemini Rials. During those days the Yemini Rial was a pure silver coin and was much in demand at the London Bullion Exchange. Young Dhirubhai would buy Rial, melt it in pure silver and sell it to bullion traders in London. In the later part of his life while talking to reporters it is believed that he said, *"The margins were small but it was money for jam. After three months, it was stopped. But I made a few lakh of rupees. I don't believe in not taking opportunities."*

Ten years later, Dhirubhai returned to India and started a business Reliance Commercial Corporation with a capital of Rs. 15000 (US $ 375). The primary business of Reliance Commercial Corporation was to import polyester yarn and to export spices. The business was setup in partnership with Champaklal Damani, his second cousin who was also there with him in Aden, Yemen.

The first office of Reliance Commercial Corporation was set up at Narsinathan Street at Masjid Bunder. It was a 350 sq. ft. room with a telephone, one table and three chairs. Initially they had two assistants to help them in their business. In 1965, Champaklal Damani and Dhirubhai Ambani ended their partnership and Dhirubhai started on his own. It is believed that both had different tempermants and different thoughts to take on business, while Champaklal was a cautious trader and did not believe in building Yarn inventories. Dhirubhai was a known risk taker and he considered that building inventories with anticipating a price rise and making some profit is good for growth. During this period, Dhirubhai and his family used to stay in a one bedroom apartment in *Jaihind Estate* in Bhuleshwar. In 1968, he moved from the chawl to an upmarket apartment at Altamount Road in South Mumbai. His first car was Premier Padmini, the Indian version of Fiat 1100, later he brought a Mercedez-Benz Car. In 1970s he brought a white Cadillac Car.

Only Vimal

Sensing good opportunity in the business of textiles, Dhirubhai started his first textile mill at Naroda, near Ahmedabad in the year 1966. Textiles were manufactured using polyester fibre yarn. Dhirubhai started the brand 'Vimal', which was named after his elder brother Ramaniklal Ambani's son Vimal Ambani. Extensive marketing of the brand 'Vimal' in India made it a household name. Franchise retail outlets were started that used to sell only 'Vimal' brand of textiles. In 1975, a Technical team from the World Bank visited Reliance Textiles' Manufacturing unit. This unit has the rare distinction of being certified as "excellent even by developed country standards" in that period.

Dhirubhai Ambani is credited with starting the equity cult in India. More than 58,000 investors from various parts of the country subscribed to Reliance's IPO in 1977. Dhirubhai was able to convince people of rural Guajrat that being shareholders of his company will only bring returns to their investment. Reliance Industries holds the distinction that it is the only Public

Limited Company whose several Annual General Meetings were held in stadiums. In 1986, The Annual General Meeting of Reliance Industries was held in Cross Maidan, Mumbai, and was attended by more than 30,000 shareholders.

In 1982, Reliance Industries was coming up with a rights issue of partly convertible debentures. It was rumoured that the company is making all efforts to ensure that the stock prices did not slide a inch. Sensing an opportunity a Bear Cartel which was a group of stock brokers from Calcutta started to short sell the shares of Reliance. To counter this, a group of stock brokers till recently referred as 'Friends of Reliance' started to buy the short sold shares of Reliance Industries on Bombay Stock Exchange. The Bear Cartel was acting with a belief that the Bulls will be short of cash to complete the transaction and would be ready for settlement under the *Badla* trading system prevalent in Bombay Stock Exchange during those days. The Bulls kept on buying and a price of Rs. 152 per share was maintained till the day of settlement. On the day of settlement the Bear Cartel was taken aback when the Bulls demanded a physical delivery of shares. To complete the transaction the much needed cash was provided to the stock brokers who had brought shares of Reliance by none other than Dhirubhai Ambani. In case of non-settlement the Bulls demanded an *Unbadla* (penalty sum) of Rs. 35 per share. With this the demand increased and the shares of Reliance shot above 180 rupees in minutes.

The settlement caused enormous uproar in the market and Dhirubhai Ambani was the undisputed king of the stock market. He proved to his detractors as to how dangerous it is to play with Reliance. The situation was completely out of control. To get a solution for this situation the Bombay Stock Exchange was closed for three business days. Authorities of Bombay Stock Exchange intervened in the matter and brought down the *Unbadla* rate to Rs. 2 with a stipulation that the Bear Cartel has to give the delivery of shares within few days. The Bear Cartel brought shares of Reliance from the market at higher price levels.

It was also realized that Dhirubhai Ambani himself supplied those shares to the Bear Cartel and earned a healthy profit out of their adventure.

After this incident many questions were raised by his detractors and the press. Not many people were able to understand as to how a yarn trader till a few years ago was able to get in so much of cash flow during the crisis.

The answer to this was provided by the then finance minister Pranab Mukherjee in the parliament. He informed the house that Non-Resident Indians (NRIs) had invested upto Rs. 220 million in Reliance during 1982-83. These investments were routed through many companies like *Crocodile*, *Lota* and *Fiasco*. These companies were primarily registered in Isle of Man. The interesting factor was all the promoters or owners of these companies had a common surname *'Shah'*. An investigation by the Reserve Bank of India in the incident did not find any unethical or illegal acts or transactions committed by Reliance or its promoters.

Over time his business has diversified into a core specialisation in petrochemicals with additional interests in tele-communications, information technology, energy, power, retail, textiles, infrastructure services, capital markets, and logistics. The company as a whole was described by the BBC as "a business empire with an estimated annual turnover of $12bn, and 85,000-strong workforce".

Despite his almost Midas Touch, Dhirubhai is known to have flexible values and an unethical streak running through him. He has been accused of having manipulated government policies to suit his own need, and has been known to be a king-maker in government elections. Although most media sources tend to speak out about business-politics nexus, the Ambani house has always enjoyed more protection and shelter from the media storms that sweep across the country.

After spending a rather healthy life Dhirubhai Ambani was admitted to the Breach Candy Hospital in Mumbai on June 24, 2002 due to a major brain stroke. This was the second stroke, the first one had occurred in February 1986 and had kept his right hand paralyzed.

He was in a state of coma for more than a week. A battery of highly efficient doctors were unable to save his life. He breathed his last on July 6, 2002, at around 11:50 P.M. (IST). His funeral procession was not only attended by business people, politicians and celebrities but also by thousands of ordinary people. His elder son, Mukesh Ambani performed the last rites as per the Hindu traditions. He was cremated at the Chandanwadi Crematorium in Mumbai at around 4:30 PM (IST) on July 7, 2002. He is survived by Kokilaben Ambani, his wife, two sons, Mukesh Ambani and Anil Ambani, and two daughters, Nina Kothari and Deepti Salgaocar.

❑

"Pursue your goal, even in difficulties. Convert difficulties into opportunities. Keep your morale high, in spite of setbacks. At the end, you are bound to succeed."

—Dhirubhai Ambani

Childhood Days

Dhirubhai was born at Chorwad, in the district of Junagarh in the western Indian state of Gujarat. Chorwad was then, as it is now, a small village about midway between the historic fort of Diu to the south and the fishing port of Porbandar to the north. Porbandar is the birthplace of Mahatma Gandhi. (Incidentally, the Gandhis and the Ambanis come from the same stock or *gotra*, the trading community of Modh baniyas.).

Dhirubhai's father, Hirachand Govardhandas Ambani, earned little as the village school teacher. He was, however, a man of simple habits and lived a measured life. Dhirubhai's mother, Jamanaben, was a thrifty woman and knew how to stretch every paisa a long way. Long years of hardship had taught her to handle with great care whatever little money Hirabhai gave her every month on the pay day.

But even her thrifty ways often failed to pull her growing family through the month. On such occasions she had to borrow small amounts of money from neighbours. She did not hide such day-to-day stark realities from her children, for she did not want to give them a false start in life.

Overall, Hirachandbhai and Jamanaben lived a life of impoverished dignity with their two daughters and three sons-Trilochanaben, Ramnikbhai, Jasuben, Dhirubhai and Natubhai. Dhirubhai was the favourite child of both Hirachandbhai and Jamanaben.

He was from his very childhood days extremely demanding, robust of health and difficult to placate. As he grew up to boyhood, he became even more vigorous, unyielding and irrepressible. He possessed immense gusto and enormous energy and was always determined to do what he wanted to do in exactly the way he wanted it done, come hell or high water, as the phrase goes. But Hirachandbhai was a fond father and seldom, if ever, spoke harshly to his children, especially to his favourite one.

Dhirubhai was precocious and highly intelligent and also as highly impatient of the oppressive grinding mill of the school classroom. Formal education was not his forte, he realized very early in life. He was essentially an outdoors boy. When asked to choose a task at home, at school or at the boys' hostel, he always chose the most strenuous task that called for immense physical energy and stamina. Not that he was poor in doing his school lessons but just that he did not enjoy all the mugging up and learning by rote which school education required those days.

As his elder brother Ramnikbhai and he grew into boyhood, Jamanaben began exhorting them to help supplement their father's meager income. "Begin earning some money," she nagged them. That angered Dhirubhai. "*Phadia, phadia su karo chho,*" he snapped at her, "*paisa no to dhanglo karees.*" (Why do you keep screaming for money? I'll make heaps of money one day.). Just to show that that was not an empty boast, he once procured a tin of groundnut oil on credit from a local whole seller and sold the oil in retail sitting on the roadside, earning a profit of a few rupees that he gave to his mother. Next, he began setting up *bhajia* fries stalls at village fairs during weekends when his school was closed.

❑

"*We can prove to the world that India can do it. That Indians are not afraid of competition. That India is a nation of achievers.*"

—*Dhirubhai Ambani*

Off to Aden

Just after Dhirubhai was through his annual matriculation examination and even before the result was out, Hirachandbhai called him home to Chorwad. Hirachandbhai had been unwell for quite some time and had grown extremely weak and frail.

"Dhiru, do you know why I have called you here?" Hirachandbhai asked his son the very night he reached home. "Well, I'll tell you. You know I have been unwell for past several months. I cannot work any more. I know you want to study further but I can't afford that any more. I need you to earn for the family. I need your money. The family needs it. You must work now. Ramnikbhai has arranged a job for you in Aden. You go there."

Dhirubhai was really interested in completing his graduation, but his ambition melted when he looked into the anxious eyes of his sick father. "I'll do as you say, Hirabhai," he said and the very next morning he left for Rajkot to get his passport. Those days Indians did not need a visa for entering Aden but there were rumours around that no visa regime was about to change any day. So he needed to hurry up before the visa rules changed. In a few days, he was in Mumbai to board the ship to Aden. It was on boarding the ship that Dhirubhai learnt from Gujarati newspaper that he had passed his matriculation examination in second division.

On reaching Aden, Dhirubhai joined office on the very day of his arrival. It was a clerk's job with the *A. Besse & Co.*, named after its French founder Antonin Besse. Those days Aden was the second busiest trading and oil bunkering port in the world after London handling over 6,300 ships and 1,500 steamers a year.

And, there in Aden, *A. Besse & Co.* was the largest transcontinental trading firm east of Suez. It was engaged in almost every branch of trading business-cargo booking, handling, shipping, forwarding, and wholesale merchandising. Besse acted as trading agents for a large number of European, American, African and Asian companies and dealt with all sorts of goods ranging from sugar, spices, foodgrains and textiles to office stationary, tools, machinery and petroleum products. Dhirubhai was first sent to the commodities trading section of the firm. Later, he was transferred to the section that handled petroleum products for the oil giant Shell.

"I learnt business at the Besse which was then the best trading firm of this side of the Suez," he used to tell friends in later years. He was quick on the uptake. He learnt the ways of commodity trading, high seas purchase and sales, marketing and distribution, currency trading, and money management. During lunch break, he roamed the bazaars of Aden where traders from numerous different continents and countries bought and sold goods worth millions of pound sterling, the then global currency, during the day.

He met traders from all parts of Europe, Africa, India, Japan and China. Aden was the biggest trading port of the times, a trading port where goods landed from all parts of the world and were dispatched to the farthest corners of different continents. Speculation in manufactured goods and commodities was rife all over the Aden bazaars.

Dhirubhai felt tempted to speculate but had no money for that and was still raw for such trading. To learn the tricks of the trade he offered to work free for a Gujarati trading firm. There he learnt accounting, book keeping, preparing shipping papers and documents, and dealing with banks and insurance companies, skills that would come handy when he launched himself into trading about a decade afterwards in Mumbai. At the Besse office during the day he polished his skills in typing and Pitman shorthand, drafting commercial letters, and composing legal documents.

At the boarding house where he lived with another twenty-five or so young Gujarati clerks and office boys, he devoted long hours of the night mastering English grammar, essay writing, current affairs and a host of subjects that took his fancy from week to week. He was the first to snatch the English, Gujarati and Hindi daily papers and weeklies as soon as they arrived by the ship every day. The Times of India, Blitz, Janmabhoomi and Navajeevan formed his favourite reading material. He also devoured all sorts of books, magazines and journals the passengers arriving from various European and Indian ports left in the ships and at the offices of various shipping agents.

"Of all the books I read so avidly those days one I remember most fondly are (Jawaharlal Nehru's) the 'Glimpses of World History' and the 'Discovery of India'," he would recall long after his Aden days. *"They were fat, big books but written in simple English and to me they opened a whole new world of adventure, of human wisdom and human folly. I began reading them not to learn world history but to practice my English but once I opened their pages their breadth of vision had me in a thrall. I used to keep a dictionary by my side when reading these books and note down every new word I came across to increase my vocabulary. Later when I used to draft letters to ministers and senior officials during my early Mumbai days, I used whole lot of quotations, phrases and impressive words from these two books."*

He also gorged on dozens of books and magazine articles on psychology that became his favourite subject for a long time. *"I learnt much from this class of my reading,"* he sometimes said, *"I learnt how we humans and animals love to be loved more than anything else, how we are driven by desire to earn the love, affection and honour of those around us, what it is to be a leader, how to motivate those whom we*

*want to attain great heights, how ideologies and interests clash and reconcile
or cancel each other.*

"*More than anything else I learnt that nothing big can ever be achieved
without money, influence and power and I also learnt that money, influence
and power alone cannot achieve anything in life, big or small, without a
certain soft, delicate, sensitive, understanding human touch in all one's
deeds and words.*"

After he thought he had learnt the basics of commodities
trading, Dhirubhai began speculating in high seas purchase
and sales of all sorts of goods. He did not have enough money
of his own for such speculative trading. So he borrowed as
much as he could from friends and small Aden shopkeepers
on terms, nobody had ever offered them. *'Profit we share and all
loss will be mine'* became his motto. During lunch break and
after office hours he was always in the local bazaar, trading in
one thing or the other.

Soon, those around him found that he had an uncanny knack
for such speculative trading. He seldom lost money in any deal.
"*I think I had an animal instinct about such trading but there was a lot of
reading and understanding of market trends behind that animal instinct
of mine. I read every bit of paper I could lay my hands on about what was
happening around the world, I listened carefully to every word uttered in
the market, picked every bit of gossip in the shipping circles and pondered
long through the night in the bed about the pros and cons of every deal I
wanted to make.*"

Meanwhile, the Shell oil refinery and the first oil harbour
came up in Aden in 1954, the year Dhirubhai returned home to
marry Kokilaben. As expected, *A. Besse & Co.* became the agents
for distribution of Shell refinery products. Dhirubhai had done
well at the office during his first five years. Now he was sent on
promotion to the oil filling station at the newly built harbour.

He liked the new job, though it was a lot more demanding
than the desk job in the commodities section. Here he had to
service the ships bunkering for diesel and lubricants. He enjoyed

visiting the ships, making friends with sailors and the engine staff, I heard from them first hand accounts of their voyages in different parts of the world of which he had until then read about only in books and magazines. And, here it was that he first began dreaming of building a refinery of his own one day.

"It was a crazy idea for a petrol pump attendant to build a refinery of his own, but that is the sort of crazy ideas I have been playing with all my life," Dhirubhai recalled at the time Reliance's 25-million ton oil refinery, the largest grassroots refinery in the world, went on stream in Jamnagar in 1999. *"I have been able to build this refinery because I decided long years ago not to settle for anything else,"* he said, *"I had heard a Yemeni proverb in Aden "la budd min Sana'a wa lau taal al-safr" (Sana'a is a 'must', however, long the journey may take). I never forgot that saying."*

By the late 1950s it became clear that the British rule in Aden would not last long in the face of growing Yemeni movement for independence supported by Gamal Abdel Nasser's revolutionary government from across the Suez. The large Indian community of Hindu and Parsee Gujaratis began preparing to move out of Aden. Some began returning home to India, while some chose to settle in Britain. Aden Indians those days were allowed to settle in Britain.

Where to go on leaving Aden was debated among the colony's settlers every day. Some of Dhirubhai's friends told him that he should migrate to London where, considering his talents, acumen and guts, he could find better opportunities of growth. At the port and on ships at Aden he often heard glowing accounts of post-war Britain and the promises of a life of much greater ease there than one could ever hope to find in India.

Dhirubhai weighed his options. By now he had saved some money and was thinking of setting up some business of his own. Although Dhirubhai's father had died in 1952, he had in the meantime been blessed with his first son, Mukesh Ambani, in April, 1957. Kokilaben and Mukesh were back home in India. The choice of opening a shop somewhere in London was tempting but he felt India was calling him home.

Those were exciting years in India. The country was in the midst of implementing the second five-year Plan which promised to build big industries, raise new big dams across many rivers, lay new roads through the length and breadth of the country, boost agricultural production to new record levels and set up a huge network of foodgrains procurement centers.

Dhirubhai with Kokilaben in Youth Days

Though by the end of 1958, the newspapers coming from India were painting a rather gloomy picture of the country's finances and foreign exchange reserves, there was also a new vigour and a new fervor in their reports of a new Rs 10,000-crore five-year Plan then under preparation. The Plan promised to open massive new opportunities for growth of the country's youth. Jawaharlal Nehru was daily exhorting the young to cast away their old ways and help build a new India. His words were stirring and roused the passions of every young Indian, especially of those living far away from the country.

Dhirubhai was now 26 years, full of youthful vigour and vitality, and filled with high hopes for himself and for the new

Pleasant marital life in later Days

India of Nehru's dreams. He just could not miss the excitement of being in India in such tumultuous times. He decided to return home, instead of going to London to live a life of ease there.

❏

*"I have trusted people and they have put their trust in me.
I have encouraged youth, and they have never let me down.
I have asked my people to take initiative and to take risks.
It has paid me rich dividends. I insist on excellence. This
helps us to be leaders. Reliance is built on some of these
principles."*
—*Dhirubhai Ambani*

Early Years in Mumbai

Sometime towards the end of 1958 Dhirubhai landed at Mumbai with little money in his pocket and absolutely no connections except a letter of introduction from a Gujarati shopkeeper in Aden to his son living in a Mumbai, chawl to let him share his room. Soon after arriving in Mumbai, Dhirubhai began exploring openings for some business within limits of his meager savings. He went to various places like Ahmedabad, Baroda, Junagarh, Rajkot and Jamnagar in Gujarat for exploring opportunities. But he felt that with the small capital he had all that he could do in these places was to set up a grocery, cloth or a motor parts shop. A shop could give him a steady income but that was not what he was looking for. He was looking for quick growth, for constant excitement of trading, and for the hustle and bustle of a busy bazaar, as in Aden.

He came back to Mumbai, settled himself, his wife and son in a two-room *chawl* and launched himself as a trader in spice setting up office under the name of Reliance Commercial Corporation. All that his office had was a table, two chairs, a writing pad, a pen, an inkpot, a pitcher for storing drinking water and a few glasses. The office had no phone but he could make and receive calls on the phone of a next-door doctor paying him a small amount for every such call. From the very first day, Dhirubhai began making rounds of Mumbai's wholesale spice market and collecting quotations of various items for bulk purchase on immediate down payment terms.

A jobless young boy known to him appeared soon after as his odd job man. An aged Muslim Methaji was brought in as a

Turned Dreams into Reality

part time clerk-cum-letterwriter-cum-accountant-cum-receptionist. From the very first day, he began sending letters in Arabic to Dhirubhai's old contacts in Aden and trading centers of the Gulf Emirates. The letters carried rates at which Dhirubhai offered to supply various commodities like spices, sugar, jaggery, betel nuts and other things.

Orders began trickling in after a few weeks, and were promptly fulfilled. Often goods were shipped even before payments arrived. Dhirubhai kept his margins low, volumes large and quality high. Those days most of the Mumbai traders paid little attention to the quality of their commodities. There was a lot of adulteration and mixing of substandard material in bulk shipments. Foreign exporters often complained that goods shipped from India were all so often a much lower quality than promised. Dhirubhai offered to forego payments in case his supplies were found below standard. That built a great reputation for him among overseas exporters. Orders began growing.

❑

"Growth has no limit at Reliance. I keep revising my vision. Only when you dream it you can do it."

—Dhirubhai Ambani

DHIRUBHAI:
TASKS AHEAD

Always Ready to Face Challenges

Dhirubhai began enlarging his basket of commodities on offer. He offered to supply anything and everything required from India.

Once an enquiry came from a Gulf trader for manure mixed topsoil for a Sheik's lawn and rose garden. It was a large order and the price offered was high. But nobody before that had ever received or fulfilled such an order.

Dhirubhai's friends told him there was no way anybody could gather so much of manure mixed topsoil in Mumbai and that too in such a short time as required. But that was the sort of challenge that always spurred Dhirubhai's nerves. Against advice of all friends, he offered to meet the order but asked the Gulf party for a bonus on top of the offered price which was conceded.

Dhirubhai gathered all unemployed youth from his neighbouring *chawls* and asked them to fan out all around Mumbai and buy all rotten dung heaps they found. A graduate in agriculture science was hired to oversee preparation of the topsoil, which was packed, transported to Mumbai and shipped to the Gulf within the given time. "*We made big money from that order, real big money,*" Dhirubhai said.

❏

Yarn Years

After a few years, the thrill of trading in commodities began to wear out. Dhirubhai began to feel that trading in commodities would not take him far enough. Just about this time he made friends with some yarn traders in the *chawl* where he lived. They told him that huge money may to be made in the yarn business.

Yarn trade was complicated, highly speculative and dominated by some big firms like *Forbes, Forbes & Gokak* that had been in import-export business since a long time. Price fluctuations in the yarn market were vast which made the business extremely risky. Besides, yarn trade required a large amount of cash.

But, if the risks were high, so were the margins for a man of daring. Dhirubhai liked that. He began frequenting the yarn market where he stood quietly at a corner during business hours and observed how the trade worked. Gradually, he began buying and selling different types of yarn, first in small quantities, then in ever-increasing volumes.

As business grew, so did his need for funds. He resorted to his Aden formula. Many of the small Gujarati building contractors, merchants and brokers were flush with funds. They used to lend their savings and surplus money at a high interest. They never lent a large sum to any single person. Dhirubhai offered them staggering rates of interest. When a deal turned out to be especially great, he topped the sum with some icing as bonus. To some others he offered his Aden terms - *"loss is mine, profit I share."*

From thereon, he had no dearth of funds. Actually, every evening builders and merchants thronged his office with huge bundles of notes to lend. He came to be known as the man with the golden touch. He now began making huge deals in yarn, often booking lots on the high seas. As business grew, he shifted to a larger office. His two brothers, Ramnikbhai and Nattubhai, and some friends from his Aden days, joined him.

Yarn trading: The beginning of Reliance Industries

Then one day someone set off a bombshell of rumour in the yarn market, a rumour that Dhirubhai had gone bust and that all those who had lent him money were sunk. Panic gripped among his lenders and the brokers who had sold him yarn but not yet received their dues. The funds involved were large. Even Dhirubhai's brothers and friends who knew the rumour was false were shaken. Dhirubhai was unaware of the entire activities. When he reached office that afternoon, he was told about the rumour and the calls that were pouring in from panicky creditors. He was advised to stay away from the office for a few days until the rumours died down.

"No," said Dhirubhai, *"My staying away from office will serve only to fuel the rumour further and embolden those who have spread the rumour.*

I better take them head on. Go out and tell everybody whom we owe any money to come to our office at four in the afternoon and take their money back. Write that on the market notice board too."

"But, Dhirubhai, where do we have the money to pay them?" asked his brothers. *"Don't you bother about that. Do as told!"* said Dhirubhai gruffly, and went off. It was not possible to arrange so much of cash so quickly. However, Dhirubhai was sure that not all his lenders were going to take their money back. A few troublemakers might, but most others would be happy just to see him there in his office. Then, as promised, sharp at four in the afternoon Dhirubhai took his chair in his office to face the creditors.

For half an hour nobody turned up. Even the phone stopped ringing up. The notice pasted at the market meeting place had had its desired effect. Once he had offered the money back, nobody wanted it any more. Quite to the contrary, several big lenders came to his office and assured him that, far from wanting their money back, they would be happy to lend him more if he needed.

That was the first vicious campaign and inspired market raid Dhirubhai faced, and overcame. He would face several similar attempts to bring him down in his long business life in later years. *"I was stepping on too many shoes then,"* he once said, *"Such fast growth as mine was bound to cause envy. It is but natural. It is human. To grow the way I have one must be ready to pass through hell, the fire of envy and opposition, criticism and attacks."*

Soon after, Dhirubhai was elected a director of the Mumbai Yarn Merchants Association. Those days there existed no rules or norms in yarn market about payments for deals made. Also, brokerage rates were arbitrary. That was a major cause of altercation among sellers, brokers and buyers. Dhirubhai moved to clear these grey areas. The association also regulated the wages of *mathadi* labourers (handcart labourers who move goods).

By this time, Dhirubhai had earned a name for himself in the Mumbai yarn market and at different handloom and powerloom centres of the country. But, recognition to him as the lion of yarn traders came when in the early sixties he introduced a new viscose-based yarn called bamber or *chamki* (shiny). The filament yarn was named *Bemberg* after an Italian company of that name which had first developed it. Bemberg sold the technology to Asahi of Japan. Bamber had a distinct shine and lustre well suited for *saris* and dress materials. Bamber filament made fabrics last longer than ordinary nylon.

While most mill-owners were yet to see the wonder that bamber could do, Dhirubhai was quick to see its attractive features for saris and dresses. He took the next flight to Japan and booked a huge lot of bamber filament for import. By the time his first bamber shipment arrived, the first few mills that had made saris and dress materials from the wonder filament were overwhelmed by the craze, customers were showing for the new-look fabric. Dhirubhai's first bamber lot sold like the proverbial hot cakes at a big premium. Over the next few months Dhirubhai had the *chamki* market in his grip. As the demand for *chamki* soared, so did Dhirubhai's profit. That was where the first big flush of capital for the future Reliance Textiles came from.

Another big flush came from a government scheme in the mid-sixties for import of nylon yarn, then much in demand, against export of rayon fabrics. Rayon, commercially developed by Sears in 1930 in America, had been made in India since 1954 and was used mainly for saris. Rayon was used for making other fabrics too. Excise duty on rayon was low and, with low Indian labour costs, rayon fabrics could be sold at competitive prices in the overseas markets.

Nylon was developed in 1938 in Germany and about the same time in America. Nylon's advent created a revolution in several consumer industries, especially in fibres and fabrics. Nylon was a synthetic fibre, the first to be drawn entirely from petrochemical, whereas rayon was derived from a natural source, plant cellulose. In the 1960s nylon was just coming into fashion in India, though in America it had gained popularity a decade earlier.

Nylon was not yet being produced in India and, as a craze for nylon fabrics, was growing in the country, it had to be imported at a considerable outflow of foreign exchange that was becoming increasingly scarce from the middle of the 1950s. Also, smuggling of nylon from neighbouring countries was growing menacingly. Because of these reasons, the government went in for the nylon for rayon scheme. Although the government scheme for import of nylon against export of rayon was a common knowledge, again Dhirubhai was the first to make use of it in a big way. He took to export of rayon fabrics in right earnest. Once again his Aden contacts came in handy. A lot of textile exports from India as also yarn imports were routed through Aden. Dhirubhai made the best use of his Aden connections. As in spices, so in rayon fabrics too he was quick in delivering orders. He also began seeding new markets in Eastern Europe that would prove to be of immense potential when he would launch himself into textiles, a few years later.

Dhirubhai was mostly outsourcing rayon fabrics those days. Outsourcing was a headache. Also, Dhirubhai felt that the nylon for rayon scheme might not last for long. He was earning huge money selling nylon yarn but he felt that he could make a lot more money if, instead of selling the yarn to mills, he himself converted the yarn into the material. The nylon craze was fast spreading from big cities to small towns and villages, thanks to Mumbai films.

So, he began playing with the idea of establishing his own independent manufacturing unit. He had built enough capital during trading in yarn to be able to launch himself into the new orbit of manufacturing. That was his first major step towards what would later come to be hailed as his farsighted strategy of 'backward integration'.

During the seven years between 1958 and 1965, Reliance Commercial Corporation (RCC) kept growing as more and more of Dhirubhai's friends and colleagues joined him. Most of them were from Aden where word had reached that Dhirubhai had done well in life and had a growing business of his own. Therefore, everybody returning home from Aden and looking for a job in Mumbai sooner or later landed at his door. He put them on to whatever job they were good at.

Most of them had little or no formal education. Only a few were matriculates and just two or three had had a college education, of whom one was a chartered accountant. All of them, however, had some grassroots work experience from their Besse days in Aden. *"I didn't need clean shirts for the sort of business I was doing,"* said Dhirubhai recalling his Bhat Bazar days, *"I needed gutsy, street smart guys with a lot of common sense and bazaar skills."*

Dhirubhai ran his team more like the head of a joint Hindu family than as a chief executive. He was friendly, flexible and forgiving in his conduct with his staff, showed understanding of human weaknesses and shortcomings, even in case of a major error of judgment, and often went out of his way to help them in their hour of need. In return, he got immense loyalty from his people.

Dhirubahi & his Family

They were more than willing and happy to do his bidding, come what may, day or night, hail or storm. They were a rough, tough and an aggressive lot in Bhat Bazar. They had full authority from Dhirubhai to act as they thought best when the need arose. *"Profit shall be ours, loss mine; credit yours, discredit mine,"* he would tell them. *"Use my name, even misuse it if necessary, but get the work done,"* he exhorted them, *"Blame it on me if things go wrong, but act and act quick!"* In a few years, he built an immensely loyal, dedicated and highly motivated team.

In the meantime, Dhirubhai's family had also grown bigger. Mukesh was now in his ninth year and going to school. So was the second son, Anil, born in 1959. Two daughters, Dipti and Nina, had arrived in 1961 and 1962, respectively. He had by now moved into a better and bigger apartment at 7, Altamount Road in South Mumbai.

❑

"My advice to young entrepreneurs is not to accept defeat in the face of odds. Challenge negative forces with hope, self-confidence and conviction. I believe that ambition and initiative will ultimately triumph. The success of the young entrepreneur will be the key to India's transformation in the new millennium."

—*Dhirubhai Ambani*

First Step Backward

When Dhirubhai decided to start a textile unit of his own, friends suggested that instead of risking all his money on a costly, new mill of his own, he should buy an old one and renovate it. His staff began looking for one around Mumbai. The first one he went to look for the Gautam Silk Mills at Goregaon, jointly owned by five brothers. Negotiations were held with the eldest who agreed on behalf of other partners to sell the mill for Rs.3 lakh. He even took a token amount of a few thousands of rupees as advance. But just when the deal was to be initialed, one of the partners' came against the agreement. *"You keep your juna dabla* (old tin),*"* Dhirubhai snorted, *"and the advance too."* He left the meeting without turning back.

Although one of his friends took him to yet another mill at Ambernath, he no longer liked the idea of acquiring an old one. He decided to set a brand new mill of his own. Not just a new one, but an absolutely brand new one, the best and the latest from the frontiers of the then available technology. *"That was the first time I decided that whatever I ever build, I would always have the best and the most advanced in technology, come what may and whatever be the cost,"* he later said, *"In all my life I've never compromised on the principle whether it was Patalganga or Jamnagar or Hazira."*

Once the decision to go in for a new factory was taken, he sent out his two brothers, Ramnikbhai and Nattubhai, and his other colleagues to search for a suitable site. Land for a mill was costly in and around Mumbai, the centre of the textile trade. Just then Ramnikbhai reported from Ahmedabad that adequate land for a factory and for any future expansion was available at a comparatively cheap rate of Rs. 8 per square yard at an industrial estate being developed by the Gujarat State Industrial Development Corporation at Naroda, close to the textile city of Ahmedabad. Only Rs. 2 a square yard was required to be paid initially, while the rest could be paid by way of easy monthly installments.

Naroda had then just been chosen for developing an industrial estate. There was only a semi-tarred road leading to the site from Ahmedabad. All around was hard, dry, barren, brush land. Even the industrial plots had not yet been marked out with *chuna* (lime), as was the practice those days. Power lines were still being erected and water pipes being laid, and only two factories (Coca Cola and Ingersoll Rand) had come up in the estate. Reliance moved in  on plot numbers 102, 103, 104 and 105, altogether measuring 5,000 square yards. Today Reliance facilities at Naroda are spread over 125 acres there.

"Naroda was not a venture but an adventure, a raw adventure," recalled Dhirubhai when a journalist asked him how he had felt when setting up his first factory. *"I had utterly no experience, nor had any of my brothers or my colleagues."* Actually, today no one will believe that Naroda was set up by a bunch of totally raw, uneducated, inexperienced young men whose only asset was their indomitable will to do *something in life.*

"Only one of my team members was an engineering graduate. Just two or three were matriculates. All the others were middle (eighth standard) pass and middle fail. Think of a team like that wanting to set up a first class textile mill."

Someone Dhirubhai met on one of his routine flights to Ahmedabad was aghast to listen that he wanted to set up a factory like that with such a team. "How are you going to do that," he asked me, "with such know-nothing street urchins?"

"Why?" Dhirubhai said, *"If Lord Rama could win Lanka with the aid of a force of monkeys, why can't I build my factory with the help of my team. Aren't they better than monkeys?"*

"I was very audacious those days. Naroda was a big dream, a great thrill, great excitement, not for me alone, but for the entire people engaged in the task. Those were the days when my entire being cried out loud with immeasurable passion what are today's popular slogans: *Hum kisi se kam nahin* and *Kuchh kar dikhana hai.* The only thought that ran through my mind all the time was *Yeh manushya janam paaya hai to kuchh karke yahan se jaana chhahiye, kuchh kar ke dikhana chhahiye."*

The Naroda project started with just six people, three of them in their thirties and two still in their twenties. Dhirubhai was the troubleshooter of the team, its conceptualiser, visualiser, leader, planner, project manager, operations coordinator, cheer person, gadfly, pincushion, hunter master, all in one. He flew in and back from Ahmedabad to Mumbai every weekend, checking the progress of the project and fixing the more troublesome nitty-gritties.

The other five included Ramnikbhai (eldest brother of Dhirubhai), who was the project-in-charge; R K Sengupta, a textile engineer who had studied in Germany and who had erected a similar factory in Colombo before Dhirubhai invited him on the team; Kishore Doshi, a science graduate just out of college; two raw hands for odd jobs, and a driver for the only car the team had for running about for dozens of permissions required from different government departments.

Dhirubhai put the team together in March 1966, showed the four barren plots allotted to Reliance and set 1 September, 1966 as the target date for starting production. "No way," said Sengupta who was the only one with the experience of having set up a factory like that.

"So find the way, make the way, and do it," growled Dhirubhai and asked, *"Tell me why you think we can't do it?"*

"Simply because we haven't even decided what machines to buy and how many, and from where!"

"Then come to Mumbai on the weekend and let us decide," said Dhirubhai.

At the RCC office, which had now been shifted to Dhobi Talao, Dhirubhai told Sen Gupta to suggest what machines to buy. *"That depends on what you want to do, how quick and with how much funds,"* he said.

Dhirubhai told him that he wanted to make the best quality nylon material in the largest possible quantities by the quickest and most efficient way possible in the world, and he wanted to start at the earliest. *"Nylon material is in great demand in India and elsewhere,"* he said, *"We can sell the material here and earn a big profit. We can export the material overseas to earn foreign exchange for the country and also earn a big profit for ourselves from the government scheme. The scheme is there now but it may not remain there for long. That is why I want the factory so quickly."*

Sengupta suggested setting up a warp knitting unit, saying that was the best way to convert one ton of nylon yarn into an equal quantity of nylon material in the quickest way possible. Dhirubhai already had that in mind. He was happy to see Sengupta coming out with the same suggestion. Once they had agreed to go in for warp knitting at Naroda, Dhirubhai told Sengupta to rush to Germany, Italy and other countries to select the machines. "We are already in May and so much has been done at the site," said Sengupta. Dhirubhai told him to do his part of the job and leave the rest to him.

Construction at Naroda started in May. Dhirubhai told Ramnikbhai to double, treble the work force, if necessary, and ensure that he had the site ready for installing the machines by the middle of August. Construction continued day and night even through the rainy months. A huge quantity of canvas sheets was ordered to cover the newly raised walls and roofs from the rain. In Europe, Sengupta selected four German made Liba warp knitting machines and a dyeing machine. A stenter machine made in India in collaboration with Germany was ordered locally.

Then, just after the machines had been ordered from Germany there was a bolt from the blue. On 6 June 1966, the rupee was devalued by 36.5 per cent. The government also wound up major export promotion schemes, including tax credits, direct subsidies and import entitlement schemes like the nylon for rayon one.

Devaluation steeply raised the project cost. Scrapping of import entitlement schemes upset the nylon for rayon plan. There were suggestions for calling a halt to the project. *"No,"* called Dhirubhai, *"We are going ahead with the project as planned."*

Work continued at a hectic pace at Naroda. Machines began arriving from early August just when the civil works were nearing completion and machine platforms were being finished. Installation of knitting machines began even as the site was being readied for the dyeing machine. However, one crucial machine had not yet been ordered. That was a boiler for generating steam. It was decided that instead of going in for a big, new boiler, a second hand, small one should be bought to save time.

Just then someone reported that a 1920 make Lancashire boiler was being dismantled at the Mumbai Dyeing plant at Patalganga to make room for a bigger, new one in its place. The discarded Bombay Dyeing boiler was bought and taken to Naroda. Everything was being done simultaneously, some on the nick of time, to beat the September deadline. The pace of work all over the site was simply maddening.

Now arose the problem of locating trained and experienced textile mill workers. Naroda was too far off in a jungle to be attractive to workers from the textile centres of big cities. With great difficulty a disparate team of 35 machine men, knitting masters, boiler operators and dyeing masters was organized from Mumbai, Calcutta and Indore. As Dhirubhai had wished and planned, production started on the four knitting machines on the morning of the target date of 1 September, 1966. It took another two months for production to stabilise.

❑

"All we have to do is to break the shackles that chain the energies of our people, and India's economy will record a quantum leap and move into a new, higher orbit of growth, competitiveness and productivity."

–Dhirubhai Ambani

Most Advanced Textile Mills

By January, 1967, Naroda factory began producing fine quality fabric, about 5,000 meters a day. Then it hit a roadblock. The fabric was fine and the prices offered were attractive. Yet nobody in the wholesale markets of Ahmedabad and Mumbai was ready to touch Reliance cloth. The wholesalers stonewalled Reliance at the instance of established big mill owners who hated to see an upstart trying to enter their exclusive club. They had many more knitting machines than Reliance. No wholesaler could afford to anger or annoy them. So they shunned all Reliance materials. For four months bales, of newly rolled out fabric kept piling up in the Reliance warehouse.

The big players in the market thought seeing no way he could beat them at the game, Dhirubhai would succumb, pack up and leave them in peace. However, Dhirubhai was not one to give up a fight once started. *"We can't beat them but we can bypass them,"* he told his people, *"Let us go directly to retailers. There is no way they can stop us from selling directly to the retailers."* In the next few days, Dhirubhai's staff fanned out all over the big cities, piling bales of Reliance fabric at the retailers' counters without asking for any receipt or advance payment, and not even seeking a promise of payment in future.

In Mumbai, Dhirubhai himself did what he told others to do. He loaded the boot of his old, Austin car at his Altamount Road flat with bales of Reliance material and drove out the city the whole day long from retailer to retailer, hawking his own goods. *"Who can sell my material better than myself I thought,"* said Dhirubhai, *"If I can sell it, so can they, that is, my people on the road; if I can't, then can't either. So, I myself took to the road."*

Just across the road where Dhirubhai lived, there was a young man of the same age whose thoughts ran the same way. He also was facing a similar wholesalers' blockade as Dhirubhai. He was then living on Peddar Road and his name was Rajneesh, Acharya Rajneesh, the Osho of the later years. His predicament was not different from Dhirubhai's. Books wholesaler had stonewalled him as cloth wholesalers had Dhirubhai. Rajneesh also was loading his newly printed books in the boot of his baby Austin car and going about the city piling them at the books retailer counters on similar terms as Dhirubhai was offering to the retail cloth merchants.

Dhirubhai and Rajneesh's cars must have passed by each other many a time during those days but, as Dhirubhai said, *"I had no time then for that sort of spiritual stuff. I was in a different universe and, anyway, I had more urgent work to do. But how happy it is to know that a mahapurush like Rajneesh was then facing a similar obstacle as I was and tackling the same way as I."*)

On reaching a retailer's shop, Dhirubhai would place his visiting card on the counter and introduce himself thus, *"My name is Dhirubhai Ambani. I am a sadakchhap* (a man from the streets) *but I want to be big one day. I want you to grow with me, though at the moment I have nothing big to offer you. My brothers, some friends and I have just set up a factory at Naroda. We make knitted fabric there. The wholesalers are boycotting our material for fear of the big mill owners. I offer this material to you. I don't want any money. You sell it. If you make money by selling our material, give me whatever and whenever you want to. Now, will you not offer me a cup of tea before I go?"*

No cloth merchant had ever in his life seen a young man get out of a car with a pile of cloth on his shoulders and introduce himself like that. They had seen many smart, amiable, outgoing salesmen but never anybody so gutsy, so daring, so open and so frank as I. They were damn impressed but would be a little wary too. Many of them doubted my bona fides. They thought that I was bluffing them; that, may be I was trying to pass off stolen goods to them. On such occasions I would tell them to call up my office or factory and check my word for themselves."

The gambit worked and worked well. Reliance cut the wholesalers out of the deal, selling directly to retailers. No retailer had ever been offered such lavish terms. Slowly and steadily Reliance material began moving in the market without any promotion, publicity or advertising. In the meantime the family had named the Reliance fabric "Vimal" meaning "pure". Vimal also happened to be the name of the first born son of the eldest of the three Ambani brothers.

As Vimal sales picked and they made good money dealing in it, many retailers in different cities stopped selling other brands. "We'll sell only Vimal, Dhirubhai," they would tell him when he visited their shops. Slowly the "Only Vimal" slogan began to emerge, though it was still some years away from the phrase being adopted as the company motto for Reliance's exclusive "Only Vimal" showrooms.

As Reliance prospered, Dhirubhai kept ploughing profits back into Naroda, adding new machines year after. The Reliance team also expanded. Most of the newcomers were young men from Aden. Others were Dhirubhai's school friends or relatives, which made Reliance sort of a big, joint family.

While most were raw hands, as had been Dhirubhai's early colleagues, many newcomers on the team were drawn from established big textile and other mills and offices. They also soon became part of the Reliance flock as Dhirubhai fired them with his zeal, bonhomie and his indomitable spirit of conquering the world. Dhirubhai, his two brothers and their nephew, Rasikbhai Meswani, who had joined them during their yarn days, formed the core team.

"The four of them made a deadly combination," said one of the old hands from Naroda, "They were a very raw, a very high strung but a very low profile people. They worked hard like hell, talked like army generals in the midst of a battlefield, never bothered about creature comforts, took quick decisions, and acted so swift that by the time you said 'okay, I'll do it,' they had done it. There was never a chance of their rivals or competitors catching them napping because they just didn't nap or let anybody around and about them nap either."

They were never content or satisfied with whatever, good, bad or better, had been done or attained yesterday or the day before. They only talked about what new or better things could be done the day, month or year next. With their feet firmly on the ground, they looked at the stars and were determined to grab them. That was the spirit they had.

And, the man who kept fuelling this spirit and energizing them and others down the line like an inexhaustible dynamo was Dhirubhai. His ambition was insatiable. He just wanted to conquer not just the world but the entire universe. Very early in his Naroda days, he began saying, *'Whatever we do, we must be the best, the number one. I hate to be number two. I hate to be the next best. I must be the best.'* It is only this spirit that inspired his Naroda and Mumbai team to raise Vimal to be the finest, best selling fashion fabric of its times.

Recalling how Dhirubhai fired the zeal of his young team members, an early Naroda groupie said, "Before going to Germany for training during early Naroda days, I went to meet Dhirubhai at the Dhobi Talao office. *Do you know Tata and Birla?'* he asked.

"Yes, I have heard of them, though I have never seen or met them."

Woh kaun log hain (Who are they)?" he asked.

"They are the two biggest industrialists in India," I replied, not knowing what he had in mind next.

"Well, you are going to Germany for training," he said, now somewhat sombre, *"So all the while you are there, keep repeating to yourself that one day we have to be bigger than Tata and Birla. But we can be bigger than them only if we master our machines. Just don't limit yourself to handling the Liba machines. Go with an open mind. Keep your eyes open. Demand to see everything, look into everything, and learn everything. Make note of all that they are doing, planning, developing.*

"They will not tell you all by themselves. You will need to ask them, needle them, and pester them. Unki jaan kha jaao (be after their life). What you learn will depend on what questions you ask. Don't be with them but just the scheduled six hours of the day. Stay there in the mill 24 hours. If necessary, sleep there. Most important: make friends while you are there. We need to have friends everywhere, if we have to grow big."

"It was only his talk that made us mad for success, mad to be the best, to be number one. We felt elevated. We had a physical sensation of being uplifted in the air. He was a tremendous leader, the sort who transforms his men from clay into steel. His was an all-consuming passion, an overarching ambition. And, of all his teammates, including his brothers, no one shared his passion more or comprehended his ambition better than his young nephew, Rasikbhai Meswani, who had joined him after passing out of school a few years before the Naroda factory was started. Apart from being his nephew, Rasikbhai was also Dhirubhai's great fan. *"We knew each other's pulse, as they say in India,"* said Dhirubhai, *"We were on the same wavelength. I did not need to use words to communicate with him, nor he to me. We could see through each other's mind. At any time, he could guess, rather sense, what I wanted to be done, how and when. The best part of it was that he didn't just guess things, he*

also acted swiftly. I put him into marketing, especially, marketing of our import entitlement yarn, and he did miracles there."

Reliance grew at a fast pace. Within four or five years of starting production, the number of warp knitting machines rose to about 20 in addition to a dozen warping machines. One German Muller raising machine was installed to give the fabric a buff effect weight, and make it smooth and soft to touch. Nine texturising machines, two circular knitting machines, four weaving looms and one screen printing machine were added just within a year. By 1972-73, the number of weaving looms rose to 154 even as ever new knitting machines kept being added to the old ones. That year started an in-house design centre, the best-equipped and the largest in India.

In 1975, a World Bank team visited 24 leading textile mills in India. The team estimated the Reliance mill to be the best in the country. "Judged in relation to developed country standards," said the team in its report to the Bank, "Only one mill, Reliance, could be described as excellent." A year later, in 1976 started a major overhaul, upgradation and expansion of all plant operations.

Yet again, in 1980 the mill was expanded, renewed and renovated with installation of 148 Sulzer weaving machines, 16 Sourer weaving machines, a large men's wear processing house, 16 Scragg texturising machines (the first POY texturising machines in India), and a large spinning Sulzer processing plant.

Then, in 1983, Dhirubhai's second son, Anil Ambani, returned home after completing his MBA from the Wharton School, Pennsylvania, USA.

He joined Reliance as co-chief executive officer at Naroda just when yet another major expansion plan was in the final stage. He got involved in the new initiative from his very first day at Naroda, though the main task Dhirubhai had assigned to him at that time was marketing. Then, between 1984 and 1996, the entire face of the Naroda mill changed with installation of

280 totally computerized water jet looms, 72 Sulzer looms, 24 motif designing Jacquard looms, 48 Dornier looms, and numerous other buffing, raising, piling machines were installed. Naroda also had the first, most modern effluent treatment plant of the country.

Naroda now became the grandest composite mill in the country where spinning, texturising, dyeing, heat setting, designing, printing, knitting, weaving, that is, everything for converting raw yarn into finished bales of fabric ready for the retail shops was done at one site. And, Reliance was now making not only saris and suiting but also all sorts of highest quality material ranging from camel wool suits to world class furnishing fabrics.

❑

"First and foremost, I owe my success and achievements to the affection, friendship and trust of millions of employees, customers, shareholders, and business associates, who have stood by me and been a major source of my strength all along."

—Dhirubhai Ambani

The Dhirubhai Legend

It did not take the throng that gathered, the tears that were shed and the tributes that were paid at Dhirubhai Ambani's funeral to prove that he had established himself as a legendary leader among industrial capitalists in India. Even when he lived he had taken on a legendary dimension.

Not surprisingly, fables about him abound, many of which were recalled by the media when he passed away on July 6, 2002. The most-quoted one was the familiar rags-to-riches story, of a determined individual who ostensibly arrived in Mumbai from Aden in the late 1950s with Rs. 500 in his pocket and went on to build a Rs.65,000-crore empire. He was also reportedly a man who learnt far more than others just by plying his trade, with instances of such knowledge varying from his reported ability to recognise the quality of yarn by the sound of its twang when held to his ear to the capability to choose the best in technology in any sector he chose to invest in. Other tales were less complimentary, such as the one that he was a person who, though himself never a politician, could make and break both politicians and governments across the country to boot. There are stories of ruthlessness, when it came to bending the rules and winning the game, that made him the success that he was.

Fables such as these, built often on a modicum of truth and sometimes from thin air, were testimony to the success of Dhirajlal Hirachand Ambani. Needless to say, as is true of all winners, in Dhirubhai's case too, individual qualities—an acute mind, a sense of the other, an element of ruthlessness and a large dose of gumption that is required to make the dash to victory - would have contributed to the end result in no small measure. But by focusing on the man and his entrepreneurial adventure, they denude his life of social context and divert attention from the specific way in which the road to success of Dhirubhai and his Reliance group was related to India's post-Independence industrial history. Dhirubhai was, after all, as much a product of his times as he was one who recognised and exploited the opportunities those times offered. That strategy needs to be studied and analysed. But the occasion demands that a beginning is made.

When Ambani began business, a few business houses whose names and history captured the progress of industrial capitalism in India monopolised Indian industry. With their organisational features, their diversified structure, their dominance of virtually every sphere of manufacturing and their control over finance, they were able to manoeuvre the regulatory system, especially the licensing system, in their favour. Their track record, their financial strength, and their ability to attract credible foreign partners and to access information from within the secretive portals of the state, ensured that they were in a position to garner more than a fair share of licences. They used these licences for new investments in areas that were expanding and were profitable. But they merely held on to them as a means to prevent the entry by others into areas which they already dominated and where the profitability of new investment was not in keeping with the high returns they had come to expect in India's protected market.

This meant that the licensing system, meant to ensure that actual investments were in keeping with planned inter-sectoral allocations, and expected to curb monopoly and prevent excessive regional concentration, failed to realise these very goals. Rather, it served as a barrier to entry that protected the traditional bases of monopoly power of the business groups that had historically dominated India's industrial scene. For newcomers like Dhirubhai Ambani, therefore, accumulation had to occur in areas outside the traditional spheres of operation of established oligopoly. He chose the synthetic fibre trade, which carried synthetic yarn from the few producers of the commodity to the vast number of composite mills and burgeoning powerloom producers that were its users. It was an area where the margins, resulting from extremely high protection, were adequate to provide a decent return to the trader as well.

To many, the subsequent investment of the surpluses accumulated in trading in textile production and the synthetic fibre industry, beginning with the first plant established in 1966, was a "natural transition". But there were many prerequisites that had to be met for that transition to be made. First, Dhirubhai needed to break through the barriers to entry that the licensing regime had put in place. Second, he needed to have at his disposal an adequate amount of own capital to ensure that he could obtain the necessary credit to make up the capital required for investment in a capital-intensive area. Third, after entry, he needed to survive the competition he would face from the established players with deep pockets operating in the field. Further, if initial success had to be built upon to generate the business colossus that Reliance is, this strategy had to be replicated in more areas than one without being marooned by wrong decisions and damaging investments.

In his effort, Dhirubhai and his team were helped by circumstances. His trading operations combined with thrift, one presumes, allowed him to muster the capital needed for his first foray into manufacturing. While this was being done, the licensing regime was itself losing its credibility, having failed to achieve its objectives of ensuring an optimal allocation of investment, of curbing monopoly and of reducing regional concentration. This made the licensing system completely adhoc and arbitrary, enabling new entrants to manoeuvre the system in their favour. It was here that Dhirubhai exercised his acumen to win favour with, manipulate and benefit from the power of the bureaucracy and the political class. This ability, which allegedly was used to garner more than a few initial benefits, won him not only the licences he wanted but also a degree of notoriety.

Finally, Ambani's success in breaking into and coming to dominate the synthetic fibre industry was related to his ability to exploit the weaknesses stemming from the uneconomic scales which the business groups had established in the synthetics area during the years of external and internal protection. Partly in order to protect the domestic raw cotton producer and partly because of a perception that synthetics are a luxury because they involve a drain of foreign exchange, polyester staple fibre (PSF) and filament yarn (PFY) were heavily protected areas.

At that time, Reliance entered the industry with official capacities of 45,000 tonnes in the case of PSF and 25,125 tonnes in the case of PFY. This would have allowed it to operate at much lower costs and earn relatively high returns and surpluses at the prevailing domestic prices.

In the initial years, the process of expansion reflected Reliance's decision to integrate vertically and concentrate on petrochemicals and downstream products. Throughout this period there were a number of features that characterised the strategy of the group:

(i) Continuous vertical integration—(a) from synthetic textiles into the manufacture of polyester fibre and filament yarn, (b) from yarn and fibres to intermediates like purified terephthalic acid and mono-ethylene glycol; and (c) further upstream into basic building blocks like paraxylene; (ii) consolidation of internal capabilities generated in this process through related horizontal diversification into petrochemical end-products such as detergent intermediates.

This strategy of committing all its investments in large capacities in closely related areas was indeed risky. But, in practice, adopting that risky strategy not only helped Reliance make major inroads into the industrial sector, but also provided it with handsome dividends. The point to note is that the strategy was not in the first instance of becoming globally competitive. Rather, it was one of making inroads into the bases of traditional oligopoly. Even if this implied that Reliance had to set up world-class facilities, the latter were not used to support an export thrust. Reliance focussed on the domestic market where revenue opportunities were not lacking, and margins were much higher, permitting the generation of huge investible surpluses. In adopting this strategy, Dhirubhai's Reliance group acquired through outright purchase the best-practice technologies in the field. With world-scale plants, Reliance proved doubly competitive: not only was it able to displace both domestic producers and international suppliers from the market at prevailing customs duty rates, but in fact it could remain competitive even when duty rates were reduced. The strategy of 'going it alone', while investing in world-scale plants based on outright purchase of technology, obviously raised domestic financing requirements substantially.

It was here that Dhirubhai exploited the other opportunity that the changing times offered. This was the possibility of mobilising money from household through the stock market. India's stockmarkets were until the 1970s dominated by the financial institutions and a few large players, with trading activity being minimal and limited to a few shares. The first instance of equity serving as an option for investment of household savings arose when foreign companies, pressured by the Foreign Exchange Regulation Act (FERA), decided to dilute their equity through sale in small lots. With 'respected' foreign corporates making an offer of equity with a credible promise of regular dividend payments, small investors made their first foray into the stock market. Seeing the opportunity thus offered, Reliance under Ambani decided to enhance its equity strength to undertake new investments by tapping stock markets. Reliance made its first public issue in 1977, when it offered a chunk of Rs.10 shares to investors. The shares opened at Rs.23 reflecting the premium that Reliance was in a position to command. In the years to come, Reliance was to exploit the market through many routes to finance its breakneck expansion, garnering in the process huge premiums on the shares of existing companies. By the end of 1992, out of a total capitalisation of Rs.34,255 crores, share premium reserves and surpluses alone accounted for Rs.7,640 crores.

With large surpluses coming from its petrochemical operations and share premium reserves and additional equity and debt coming from the markets, Reliance was in a position to finance the rapid growth which took it to its current position as one among the leading business groups in India. Late in that process Reliance too decided to take the route of becoming a diversified conglomerate, entering unrelated areas like telecommunications, power and financial services.

It is indeed true that the growth and success of Reliance reflect the vision and the entrepreneurial skills of its founder. But they also epitomise the internal process of restructuring that Indian industry had begun to go through as the earlier system of regulation lost its credibility and was being gradually diluted. If Reliance had shown the way to others in that environment, India would perhaps have produced more globally competitive indigenous business groups. Unfortunately, before that process could gain momentum and be given a chance, the government opted for its current strategy of reform in which international rather than new or restructured Indian firms are coming to dominate the industrial sector.

(Courtesy: FRONTLINE)

❏

"The problem with Indians is that we have lost the habit of thinking big!"

—Dhirubhai Ambani

DHIRUBHAI:
A LEGEND

A Real Genius

In a career spanning four decades, Dhirubhai Ambani achieved the most that has ever been achieved by any industrialist in India.

He built India's largest enterprise in the private sector. That enterprise generates, at the last count, well over Rs 70 billion cash surplus a year. He had created a sustainable organisation.

He had institutionalised the key factors that have contributed to his success. These can be summarised as a penchant for global benchmarking, intense cost consciousness, determined pursuit of goals, flawless implementation, and the will to dominate.

He challenged the existing paradigm. He was seen to bend rules. And he certainly set a scorching pace for growth. He redefined project financing. He took the art of negotiations to new heights. His decisions on investment and disinvestment were far-sighted and always proved right.

Dhirubhai was a management institution, which taught many valuable lessons. Indian business could too benefit from his teachings.

In 1985, he had shared his optimism for the petrochemical field. He said that this industry converts oil and gas that come out of the ground. This cannot be stopped, until converted into materials, including polyester-based clothing, which his company was already making at that time.

His mantra was to keep the cost low, so as to garner volumes. He said that he would sell polyester below the cost of *moongfalli* (peanuts). Soon his words turned prophetic, as the global polyester prices fell dramatically below the price of peanuts!

Since he knew it would happen, he set up the plant and financed it with an eye on the cost element. He was simply obsessed with keeping costs to the bare minimum. Towards this end, he depended on technology, superior project management, and his ability to raise money at competitive rates. He employed whatever tactics were needed to achieve these goals.

From the very beginning, all his projects were benchmarked to the best in the world. The minimum economic size of projects and the appropriateness of the technology were key elements that determined the basic viability of his ventures.

He came across the vexatious government regulations that threatened to prevent him from achieving his economic objective. He then understood that government policies were the key to achieving his business goals.

He simply redefined the boundaries of business domain, including the government relationship as part and parcel of his business paradigm. To him, ends were sacrosanct. He had to find a way to reach the ambitious goals that he set for himself.

His vision guided him, both to make and, as importantly, withdraw from business choices. His calls on almost all his new ventures have been lauded by the industrial community. However, not enough attention has been paid to his strategic withdrawals.

The neat, painless exit from the textile manufacturing has not been well appreciated. After charting the course of backward integration into petrochemicals, Reliance achieved a position of domination pretty quickly. This business grew and overtook the textile business contribution, setting the stage for the exit.

. Behind this move was Dhirubhai's right call on the need to exit the troubled textile industry, without getting hurt.

While his tenacity in pursuing goals was legendary, he also showed remarkable astuteness in climbing down on the L&T issue. He avoided a potentially expensive battle for the control of L&T, which most people thought was uncharacteristic of Dhirubhai.

However, the effect of such a battle on his company would most probably have been debilitating. To him, Reliance was the ultimate possession, and it had to be protected from all dangers, including his own will and whim. The success factors in Dhirubhai's career is this uncompromising dedication with which he served Reliance.

He displayed an amazingly rare ability to influence people. Be they his own sons, the folks that worked for him, his customers, his traders, financiers or indeed the man on the street: Mukesh and Anil Ambani never tired of quoting their father, incessantly, all these years. It stemmed from his genuine desire to include people in his schemes.

When he talked about selling polyester below the price of peanuts, or when he brewed his schemes for raising money from millions of investors, he always spoke of people, as a ruler of his subjects.

He was never satisfied with plans or projects that would touch a small number of people. He often said, one out of 10 people in the world that bought anything in their life, lived in India. It costs almost as much to do business with 2,000 people, as with 20,000.

For instance, raising Rs 100 crore (Rs 1 billion) or Rs 500 crore (Rs 5 billion) probably will entail almost the same cost. Putting these two philosophies together, he would say, raise Rs 500 crore (Rs 5 billion), and do something useful with that money for the people.

His genius lay in always figuring out a win-win solution, producing a spectacular buy-in from the people he dealt with.

It is appropriate to bring this facet of his success to focus because there are few industrial houses whose workforce has consistently displayed such high levels of purposefulness, productivity, flexibility and dedication, as one had seen in the Reliance group.

The best testament to this argument was the fact that this group had lost the lowest number of days due to labour unrest in the country, despite becoming the largest private sector company, while logging one of the best labour productivity measures.

The other fascinating aspect of his developmental efforts is the complete alignment of his organisation with his vision and inculcation of his behaviour.

Almost everyone whom you met in the Reliance group was a confident and aggressive man.

It would be a great case study to chronicle his lifetime achievements, especially for the policy makers. In spite of every possible restriction one could think of, Dhirubhai set up the country's largest company in a very short span of time.

.Even the laudable achievements of the Reliance group during the controlled regime have been dwarfed by the growth during the liberalised nineties.

It shows the degree of suppression that those economic policies had imposed on the progress of the nation. And hopefully current environment will steward more astutely to encourage industrial progress and entrepreneurship, to make a thousand more Dhirubhais bloom in this country.

❑

"We must forge a new partnership for a great India. A strong and constructive partnership between industry, government and society."

—Dhirubhai Ambani

Famous Quotes of Dhirubhai

The man with a clear vision

From the very beginning Dhirubhai was seen in high-esteem. His success in the petro-chemical business and his story of rags to riches made him a cult figure in the minds of Indian people. As a quality of business leader he was also a motivator. He gave few public speeches but the words he has spoken are still remembered for their value.

- True entrepreneurship comes only from risk-taking.

- Pursue your goal, even in difficulties. Convert difficulties into opportunities. Keep your morale high, in spite of setbacks. At the end, you are bound to succeed.

- My advice to young entrepreneurs is not to accept defeat in the face of odds. Challenge negative forces with hope, self-confidence and conviction. I believe that ambition and initiative will ultimately triumph. The success of the young entrepreneur will be the key to India's transformation in the new millennium.

- Dhirubhai will go one day. But Reliance's employees and

shareholders will keep it afloat. Reliance is now a concept in which the Ambanis have become irrelevant.

- I have trusted people and they have put their trust in me. I have encouraged youth, and they have never let me down. I have asked my people to take initiative and to take risks. It has paid me rich dividends. I insist on excellence. This helps us to be leaders. Reliance is built on some of these principles.

- The secret of Reliance's success was to have ambition and to know the minds of men.

- Growth has no limit at Reliance. I keep revising my vision. Only when you dream it you can do it.

- The problem with Indians is that we have lost the habit of thinking big!

- We can prove to the world that India can do it. That Indians are not afraid of competition. That India is a nation of achievers.

- I dream India of becoming a great economic superpower.

- We must forge a new partnership for a great India. A strong and constructive partnership between industry, government and society.

- We must always go for the best. Do not compromise on quality. Reject if it is not the best — not only the best in India, but globally.

- If India wants to be a great nation, we must have courage to trust. This is my sincere belief.

- All we have to do is to break the shackles that chain the energies of our people, and India's economy will record a quantum leap and move into a new, higher orbit of growth, competitiveness and productivity.

- I can never fully repay the debt I owe to Mumbai. To all of you. My past was shaped in Mumbai.

- For those who dare to dream, there is a whole world to win!

- I am deaf to the word 'no.'

- I am 100 per cent pro-liberalisation. I do not think any industrialist is against it. But we should protect our industries, from unfair competition.

- There is no question about that (retirement). Business is my hobby. It is not a burden to me. In any case, Reliance now can run without me.

- I give least importance to being Number one. I consider myself to be fortunate in this position and would like to contribute to nation building in some way.

- Does making money excite me? No, but I have to make money for my shareholders. What excites me is achievement, doing something difficult. In this room extraordinary things must happen.

- Think big, think fast, think ahead. Ideas are no one's monopoly.

- Our dreams have to be bigger. Our ambitions higher. Our commitment deeper. And our efforts greater. This is my dream for Reliance and for India.

- First and foremost, I owe my success and achievements to the affection, friendship and trust of millions of employees, customers, shareholders, and business associates, who have stood by me and been a major source of my strength all along.

- I believe that the success of Reliance cannot be attributed to the qualities and achievements of one individual, or even a group of individuals, but has to be viewed as a triumph of process, and a spirit that binds the entire Reliance family together.

- I consider myself a pathfinder. I have been excavating the jungle and making the road for others to walk. I like to be the first in everything I do.

- I, as school kid, was a member of the Civil Guard, something like today's NCC. We had to salute our officers who went round in jeeps. So I thought one day I will also ride in a jeep and somebody else will salute me.

- My fulfillment lies in the satisfaction of every member of the Reliance family, comprising thousands of workers, managers, business associates and over five million shareholders. Being instrumental in creating wealth for over 5 million Indian families, and bringing prosperity and well being to their life is the best source of satisfaction and joy for me.
- Give the youth a proper environment. Motivate them. Extend them the support they need. Each one of them has infinite source of energy. They will deliver.
- You do not require an invitation to make profits.
- If you work with determination and with perfection, success will follow.
- Between my past, the present and the future, there is one common factor: Relationship and Trust. This is the foundation of our growth.
- We bet on people.
- Meeting the deadlines is not good enough, beating the deadlines is my expectation.
- Don't give up, courage is my conviction.
- We cannot change our rulers, but we can change the way they rule us.
- Roll up your sleeves and help. You and your team share the same DNA.
- Be a safety net for your team.
- Always be the silent benefactor. Don't tom-tom about how you helped someone.
- Dream big, but dream with your eyes open.
- Leave the professional alone!
- Change your orbit, constantly!
- Money is not a product by itself, it is a by-product, so don't chase it.

❑

Success is all that Matters

Ultimately, success is all that matters. That was the credo firing the spirit of Dhirubhai Ambani.

Dhirubhai's life was, indeed, a thumping success story of a small town boy building a giant corporation that propelled him into the ranks of the world's richest men by the time of his death.

In Dhirubhai's view of the world of business, the end justified the means. Not something that everyone would agree with. But Dhirubhai swore by this dictum and he proved the point in his own lifetime. He built a $12-billion company from scratch. He was the prime force in introducing the equity cult in the country.

His biggest achievement, however, is something that cannot be quantified—he infused the spirit of business among an entire generation of Indians who were inspired by his rags-to-riches story. He was a living motif for how inspiration coupled with hard work and the 'can-do' spirit can take one to great heights.

Being a Modh Bania, Dhirubhai was endowed with sharp business acumen and a spirit of adventure. But more than this in-born trait, there were three characteristics that set Dhirubhai apart in the conservative world of Indian business.

First, his phenomenal risk-taking ability that was far higher than other contemporary businessmen. He was a born risk-taker and believed in taking on and managing calculated risks.

When he founded Reliance Commercial Corporation in 1958, the forerunner of Reliance Industries as we now know it, Dhirubhai had just returned to India from Aden, Yemen, with his toddler-son, Mukesh, and his wife, Kokilaben, who was expecting their second child, Anil (born in 1959). It required a man of immense guts to sink his life-time savings of about $3,000 in the business of trading spices, betel nuts, cotton and viscose textiles.

Dhirubhai with one of his grand-children

In fact, Dhirubhai showed early signs of his risk-taking ability back in Aden when he was an employee of Besse & Co. Legend has it that the young Dhirubhai once took a bet that he could dive off the ship on which he was working in the harbour and swim to the shore in shark-infested waters. The bet? An ice-cream. He got it.

It is this same risk-taking ability that helped him when he ventured into textile manufacturing in 1966 within a year of buying out his original partner in the yarn business, Champaklal Damani. Ditto when he ventured into the backward integration project of setting up a plant to produce fibre intermediate, purified terephthalic acid (PTA) in the mid-80s—he was taking on established businesses and business-men. In fact, much of his fund-raising for the large capital-intensive projects that his group was involved in the 80s and 90s was underlined by tremendous risk.

Second was his firm belief that business is nothing but a web of relationships and obligations. Success depended on the right contacts in the right places and Dhirubhai perfected this to a fine art. This was a pre-requisite in the India of controls and permits where the bureaucrats and politicians sitting in New

Delhi determined the fate of your business down in Kanyakumari. Dhirubhai understood this early and directed his energies in cultivating the powers that be. His was the Indian version of American business lobbying.

, He believed in proactive moves rather than reacting to Government policy that is what his contemporaries were doing. This capacity to 'manage the environment' would be responsible for the dark spots that any chronicler of the Reliance group's evolution would encounter.

. Finally, his ability to see the larger picture and think big. Even in the 80s, Dhirubhai could see that he needed to integrate himself across the entire petrochemical chain to survive and grow. But for this vision, Reliance Textiles (as Reliance Industries was then known) would have remained just another textile company and would have vanished along with several others of its ilk in the liberalised nineties. He not only set up a PTA plant but ventured further backwards into naphtha cracking to enter the lucrative commodity plastics business.

The conception of the 7.5-million-tonne Hazira petrochemicals complex of Reliance Industries can only be termed as audacious for its times. It was done in the late 80s & early 90s when India had seen very few projects of such scale and genre. It is a tribute to the vision of the man that Hazira project has been rivalled only by yet another of his own creations, the 27-million-tonne refinery project at Jamnagar.

If today Reliance Industries strides as a colossus across the petrochemical sector it is due to that early vision of Dhirubhai. The ways and means he adopted to achieve that vision may not be something everybody would agree with but the dream itself was faultless.

Dhirubhai introduced innovative funding strategies such as the $100-year loan or the ingeniously designed triple option convertible debentures for the refinery project. The projects generated tremendous number of jobs, by themselves and in downstream sectors. The petrochemicals project made the country almost self-sufficient in plastics and synthetic fibre even as the refinery obviated petroleum product imports.

Dhirubhai's life was as colourful as the turbans and sarees of his native place. In media discussions and talk-shows, in stock market circles and in the industry, the mention of his name and his creation, the Reliance group, generates tremendous enthusiasm and will continue to do so.

It is sad indeed that Dhirubhai did not live long enough to see Reliance's own retail petrol outlets come up. To operate the pump in one such outlet would have been the ultimate achievement for the man who began his life managing the Shell refuelling operation at a military base in far-off Aden long time ago.

❑

"Does making money excite me? No, but I have to make money for my shareholders. What excites me is achievement, doing something difficult. In this room extraordinary things must happen."

—Dhirubhai Ambani

From Rags to Riches

He achieved what almost everybody would have considered impossible. In a life spanning 69 years, he built from scratch India's largest privately controlled corporate empire. Dhirajlal Hirachand better known as Dhirubhai Ambani would often say that success was his biggest enemy. He was a man who aroused extreme responses in others. Either you loved him or you hated him. There was just no way you could have been indifferent to this amazing entrepreneur who thought big, acted tough, knew how to bend rules or have rules bent for him. He was a visionary as well as a manipulator, a man who communicated with the rich and the poor with equal felicity, who was generous beyond the call of duty with those whom he liked and utterly ruthless with his rivals—a man of many parts, of irreconcilable contrasts and paradoxes galore.

Dhirubhai Ambani expired at Mumbai's Breach Candy Hospital where he had been admitted after he suffered a vascular stroke. This was his second stroke—the first had occurred more than sixteen years earlier, in February 1986, leaving the right side of his body paralysed. At his cremation, the well-heeled rubbed shoulders with the ordinary. No Indian businessman ever attracted the kind of crowd that Dhirubhai did on his last journey. After his cremation on the evening of his elder son Mukesh reminded those gathered on the occasion that in 1957, when Dhirubhai arrived in Mumbai from Aden in Yemen, he had only Rs 500 in his pocket.

He was not exactly a pauper since Rs 500 meant much more than what the amount means in this age. Nevertheless, one could not ask for a more spectacular 'rags-to-riches' tale. The second son of a poorly paid school-teacher from Chorwad village in Gujarat, he stopped studying after the tenth standard and decided to join his elder brother, Ramniklal, who was working in Aden at that time. (Not surprisingly, Dhirubhai ensured that his two sons went to premier educational institutions in the US—Mukesh was educated at Stanford University and Anil at the Wharton School of Business.)

The first job Dhirubhai held in Aden was that of an attendant in a gas station. Half a century later, he became chairman of a company that owned the largest oil refinery in India and the fifth largest refinery in the world, that is, Reliance Petroleum Limited which owns the refinery at Jamnagar that has an annual capacity to refine up to 27 million tonnes of crude oil.

When he died, the Reliance group of companies that Dhirubhai led had a gross annual turnover of Rs 75,000 crore

Mukesh & Anil with Dhirubhai

or close to US $ 15 billion. The group's interests include the manufacture of synthetic fibres, textiles and petrochemical products, oil and gas exploration, petroleum refining, besides telecommunications and financial services. In 1976-77, the Reliance group had an annual turnover of Rs 70 crore. Fifteen years later, this figure had jumped to Rs 3,000 crore. By the turn of the century, this amount had skyrocketed to Rs 60,000 crore. In a period of 25 years, the value of the Reliance group's assets had jumped from Rs 33 crore to Rs 30,000 crore.

The textile tycoon's meteoric rise was not without its fair share of controversy. In India and in most countries of the world, there exists a close nexus between business and politics. In the days of the licence control raj Dhirubhai, more than many of his fellow industrialists, understood and appreciated the importance of 'managing the environment', a healthy sign for keeping politicians and bureaucrats happy. He made no secret of the fact that he did not have an ego when it came to paying obeisance before government officials—be they of the rank of secretary to the Government of India or a lowly peon.

Long before Dhirubhai entered the scene, Indian politicians were known to curry favour with businessmen—licences and permits would be farmed out in return for handsome donations during election campaigns. The crucial difference in the business-politics nexus lay in the fact that by the time the Reliance group's fortunes were on the rise, the Indian economy had become much more competitive. Hence, it was insufficient for those in power to merely promote the interests of a particular business group; competitors had to simultaneously be put down. This was precisely what happened to the rivals of the Ambanis.

While Dhirubhai did not have too many scruples when it came to currying favour with politicians and bureaucrats, what cannot be denied is the fact that perhaps no businessman in India attracted the kind of adulation he did. He was more than just a legend in his lifetime. He successfully convinced close to four million citizens, most of them belonging to the middle class, to invest their hard-earned savings in Reliance group companies. He was fond of describing Reliance shareholders as 'family members' and the group's annual general meetings acquired the atmosphere of large melas attended by hordes.

What cannot also be refuted is the fact that the Reliance group believed in rewarding its shareholders handsomely. Much of the credit for the spread of the so-called 'equity cult' in India in recent years should rightfully go to Dhirubhai, even if the Reliance group was often accused of manipulating share prices.

When, after having spent eight years in Aden, Dhirubhai returned to Mumbai, his lifestyle was akin to that of any ordinary lower middle class Indian. In 1958, the year he started his first small trading venture, his family used to reside in a one room apartment at Jaihind Estate in Bhuleshwar. After trading in a range of products, primarily spices and fabrics, for eight years, Dhirubhai achieved the first of the many goals he had set for himself when he became the owner of a small spinning mill at Naroda, near Ahmedabad. He did not look back.

He decided that unlike most Indian businessmen who borrowed heavily from financial institutions to nurture their entrepreneurial ambitions, he would instead raise money from the public at large to fund his industrial ventures. In 1977, Reliance Industries went public and raised equity capital from tens of thousands of investors, many of them located in small towns. From then onwards, Dhirubhai started extensively promoting his company's textile brand name, Vimal. The story goes that on one particular day, the Reliance group chairman inaugurated the retail outlets of as many as 100 franchises.

Indira Gandhi returned to power in the 1980 general elections and Dhirubhai shared a platform with the then prime minister of India at a victory rally. He had also become very close to the many minister of the cabinet. He realised that it was crucial to be friendly with politicians in power, especially at a time when the group had embarked on an ambitious programme to build an industrial complex at Patalganga to manufacture synthetic fibres and intermediates for polyester production.

In 1982, Dhirubhai created waves in the stock markets when he took on a Kolkata-based cartel of bear operators that had sought to hammer down the share price of Reliance Industries. The cartel badly underestimated the Ambani ability to fight back. Not only did Dhirubhai manage to ensure the purchase of a million shares that the bear cartel offloaded, he demanded physical delivery of shares. The bear cartel was rattled. In the process, the bourses were thrown into a state of turmoil and the Bombay Stock Exchange had to shut down for a couple of days before the crisis was resolved.

The mid-eighties were a period during which the Reliance group got locked in a bitter turf battle with Bombay Dyeing headed by Nusli Wadia. The two corporate groups were producing competing products—Reliance was manufacturing purified terephthalic acid (PTA) and Bombay Dyeing, di-methyl terephthalate (DMT). Wadia lost the battle.

1986 was a crucial year for Dhirubhai. He suffered a stroke in February that year.

Things got difficult for the Ambanis after V.P. Singh became prime minister in December 1989. In 1990, government-owned financial institutions like the Life Insurance Corporation and the General Insurance Corporation stonewalled attempts by the Reliance group to acquire managerial control over Larsen and Toubro, one of India's largest construction and engineering companies. Sensing defeat, the Ambanis resigned from the board of the company after incurring large losses. Dhirubhai, who had become L&T chairman in April 1989, had to quit his post.

Once again, in an ironical twist of fate, more than eleven years later, the Reliance group suddenly sold its stake in L&T to Grasim Industries headed by Kumaramangalam Birla. This transaction too attracted adverse attention. Questions were raised about how the Reliance group had increased its stake in L&T a short while before the sale to Grasim had taken place. The watchdog of the stock markets, the Securities and Exchange Board of India (SEBI) instituted an inquiry into the transactions following allegations of price manipulation and insider trading. Reliance had to later cough up a token fine imposed by SEBI.

The plethora of scandals and controversies surrounding the Reliance group left Dhirubhai's supporters completely unmoved. His supporters would argue that there was no businessman in India whose track record was lily-white. Had the textile tycoon himself not acknowledged once to *Time* magazine that he was no Mother Teresa, they would ask.

A senior journalist pointed out that the Reliance group accounts for three per cent of India's gross domestic product (GDP), five per cent of the country's exports, 10 per cent of the Indian government's indirect tax revenues (excise and customs duties), 15 per cent of the weight of the sensitive index of the Bombay Stock Exchange and 30 per cent of the total profits of all private companies in the country put together.

Dhirubhai's supporters like to recall instances of his 'common touch' and his ability to interact with individuals from different walks of life. In 1983, he had hosted a lunch for 12,000 of his company's workers on the occasion of the marriage of his younger daughter Dipti. The departed Reliance group patriarch would often wonder aloud that if he could achieve what he did in a lifetime, why could a thousand Dhirubhais not flourish. He was sure that there were at least one thousand individuals like him in the country who would dare to dream big. And if all these entrepreneurs could achieve their ambitions, India would become an economic superpower one day, he would remark.

Dhirubhai's managerial skills were undoubtedly exceptional and he would repose his faith in professionals, many of whom had earlier worked in much-maligned public sector organisations. Whether it was the building of the petroleum refinery at Jamnagar in three years at a capital cost that was 30 per cent lower than comparable projects, or the restarting of the Patalganga plant in one month's time after sudden flood had occurred in July 1989, the Reliance management team displayed their competence on many occasions.

❏

"My fulfillment lies in the satisfaction of every member of the Reliance family, comprising thousands of workers, managers, business associates and over five million shareholders. Being instrumental in creating wealth for over 5 million Indian families, and bringing prosperity and well being to their life is the best source of satisfaction and joy for me."

—Dhirubhai Ambani

DHIRUBHAISM: A NEW CONCEPT

A Whole New 'ISM'

Dhirubhai Ambani was no ordinary leader. He was a man who gave management a whole new *'ism'*.

There is a new "ism" that I've been adding to the vast world of words for quite a while now. Because, without exaggeration it's a word for which no synonym can do full justice: 'Dhirubhaism'.

Inspired by the truly phenomenal Dhirubhai Ambani, it denotes a characteristic, tendency or syndrome as demonstrated by its inspirer. Dhirubhai, on his part, had he been around, would have laughed heartily and declared, "Small men like me don't inspire big words!"

There you have it—now that is a classic Dhirubhaism, the tendency to disregard one's own invaluable contribution to society as significant.

Everyone who knew Dhirubhai well will have his or her own little anecdote that illustrates his unique personality. He was a person whose heart and head both worked at peak levels, all the time. And that resulted in a truly unique and remarkable work philosophy, which is called here as *Dhirubhaism*.

Let us feel this new *'ism'* with a few examples:

Dhirubhaism No 1: Roll up your sleeves and help. You and your team share the same DNA. Reliance, during Vimal's heady days had organized a fashion show at the Convention Hall, at Ashoka Hotel in New Delhi.

As usual, every seat in the hall was taken, and there were an equal number of impatient guests outside, waiting to be seated. At that time of chaos Dhirubhai was at the door trying to pacify the guests.

Dhirubhai at that time was already a name to reckon with and a VIP himself, but that did not stop him from rolling up his sleeves and diving in to rescue a situation that had gone out of control. Most bosses in his place would have driven up in their swank cars at the last moment and given the manager a piece of their minds. Not Dhirubhai.

When things went wrong, he was the first person to sense that the circumstances would have been beyond his team's control, rather than it being a slip on their part, as he trusted their capabilities implicitly. His first instinct was always to join his men in putting out the fire and not crucifying them for it. Sounds too good a boss to be true, doesn't he? But then, that was Dhirubhai.

Dhirubhaism No 2: Be a safety net for your team. There used to be a time when agency Mudra was the target of some extremely vicious propaganda by Reliance peers, when on almost daily basis business ethics were put on trial. Dhirubhai didn't care much.

But one day, during a particularly nasty spell, he gently asked the concerned people if they needed any help in combating it. That did it. That was all the help that needed.

Dhirubhaism No 3: The silent benefactor. This was his another remarkable trait. When he helped someone, he never ever breathed a word about it to anyone else. There have been none among us who haven't known his kindness, yet he never went around broadcasting it.

. He never used charity as a platform to gain publicity. Sometimes, he would even go to the extent of not letting the recipient know who the donor was. Such was the extent of his generosity. "Expect the unexpected" just might have been coined for him.

Dhirubhaism No 4: Dream big but dream with your eyes open. His phenomenal achievement showed India that limitations were only in the mind. And that nothing was truly unattainable for those who dreamed big.

Not only did he dream big, he taught all to do so too. He often said, "It's difficult but not impossible!" And he was right.

Dream with your eyes open

When it came to advertise and popularize the Vimal brand, Dhirubhai thought big, a rather innovative idea. Both in size and scope Vimal's fashion shows were unprecedented in the country. Grand showroom openings, stunning experiments in print and poster work all combined to give the brand a truly benchmark image. But way back in 1980, no one would have believed it could have ever been possible.

But though he dreamed big, he was able to clearly distinguish between perception and reality and his favourite phrase "dream with your eyes open" underlined this.

He never let preset norms govern his vision, yet he worked night and day familiarizing himself with every little nitty-gritty that constituted his dreams constantly sifting the wheat from the chaff. This is how, as he put it, even though he dreamed, none of his dreams turned into nightmares. And this is what gave him the courage to move from one orbit to the next despite tremendous odds.

Dhirubhai was indeed a man of many parts, as is evident. Surely there are many people who display some of the traits mentioned above, in their working styles as well, but Dhirubhai was one of those rare people who demonstrated all of them, all the time.

And that's what made him such a phenomenal team builder and achiever. Yes, we all need "Dhirubhaism" in our lives to remind us that if it was possible for one person to be all this and more, we too can. And like him, go on to achieve the impossible too.

Dhirubhai Ambani leaves behind a strong legacy of thinking big and doing the impossible.

❑

"We must always go for the best. Do not compromise on quality. Reject if it is not the best — not only the best in India, but globally."

—*Dhirubhai Ambani*

The Entrepreneur Par Excellence

Dhirubhai Ambani, the entrepreneur who emerged as the tallest industrial leader in India, transformed the industrial landscape just as Jamshed Ji Tata and G. D. Birla did in their times. Starting his career in Aden earning just $6 a month, he raised the Reliance Group from the scratch to a $13-billion empire and a Fortune-500 company.

Dhirubhai leaves behind a strong legacy of thinking big and doing the impossible. He was not just a visionary beyond par but also an achiever. He was the architect of the equity culture in India. His competitors feared and respected him alike. International media credits him for the competence he developed for 'getting round the regulators'. Sure he did find a way to cut the bureaucratic labyrinth, but only to bypass restrictive licensing practices of those times.

Since liberalisation began about a decade ago, manufacturing has been facing a rough weather. While China has become a powerhouse of the manufacturing sector, Indian businessmen failed to take advantage of their entrepreneurial spirits to create wealth. India, therefore, needs courageous people who can follow Dhirubhai's example to create internationally competitive industries. What sorts of businesses these could be and what would be the characteristics of people who are thought of worthy successors to Dhirubhai?

The future of Indian business largely depends on how far Indian businessmen would be able to compete in the international arena. While in the licence-permit-quota raj, family-owned businesses and conglomerates flourished, in the next decade, regulatory regimes would be further relaxed. Businesses would have to develop the competencies of dealing with the critical success factors in an atmosphere of de-regulation and lower import barriers, globalisation, rapid technological change and fast-changing customers' preferences. Entrepreneurs would have to work overtime to align their practices, philosophies of conducting day-to-day affairs in tune with the international requirements and norms.

Localisation of products or services to satisfy different tastes of customers in different markets will be one of the key assets to win the battle in the marketplace. In such circumstances, any ambitious Indian businessman will have to find a niche and confine himself to just one or two lines of businesses to create a globally competitive outfit. South Korea's Chaebols, which have been shedding businesses, are no longer successful in the global market. Multi-business groups, such as ABB, Tyco, Fiat, Daewoo have all been in the news for the wrong reasons. They are having problems of one type or another.

Only GE remains at the top, as it has a philosophy of picking up and retaining businesses, which are either No 1 or 2 in their industry.

Depending on the ground realities, the changing landscape of business and opportunities in the domestic and international markets, a visionary like Dhirubhai will choose the right kind of business to enter, where he will develop a competitive advantage. Emulating personal qualities of Dhirubhai will also require developing a vision and a roadmap for creating a high-profile industry. He should be able to make a sound judgement of the approaching revolution and develop all the right strategies for growth.

Any examples to follow? Worth emulating are Finnish Nokia and South Korea's Samsung Electronics, which have become world-class in the last decade, capturing markets around the world. Not all that long ago, Nokia manufactured diapers and rubber boots. But Jorma Ollila, the CEO, turned around the company and found a niche in electronics, manufacturing mobile handsets, with a global market share of around 40 per cent now.

Similarly, Samsung Electronics, which manufactured 12 inches Black & White TV sets under Sanyo label in the 1970s, is aggressively riding the technology wave and specialising in electronics business, which today constitutes 25 per cent of the turnover and 65 per cent of the profits of the Samsung group. Its objective is to become like Sony in the international market.

We are living in the age of Toyotas, Hondas, Microsofts and Canons, all focussed in their single lines of businesses and, doing well, even in the downturn.

The real tribute to Dhirubhai would be paid, if India produces many entrepreneurs like him, who energise the manufacturing industry in India by setting personal examples and creating world-class businesses, worthy of Fortune 500 listing.

❏

"I am 100 per cent pro-liberalisation. I do not think any industrialist is against it. But we should protect our industries, from unfair competition."

—Dhirubhai Ambani

A Tycoon of All Seasons

Even a week after he slipped into coma following a brain stroke, the number of visitors inquiring about Dhirubhai Ambani's health had not diminished. Indian politicians, film stars, industrialists...they had all been to the Breach Candy hospital in south Mumbai.

But what surprised security guards at the hospital was the large number of concerned commoners walking in to ask about their favorite Indian businessman, 69, before he passed away on July 6, 2002.

And why not?

Every fourth Indian equity investor holds shares in Reliance, the business group the former Shell petrol pump attendant floated in 1977. A lowly employee of the oil giant in Aden, Yemen, Ambani dreamt of owning his own oil company one day. His is an amazing rags-to-riches story, the stuff of which legends are made.

In 1958, at the age of 25, he had come back to Mumbai and invested 15,000 rupees to start a firm exporting spices and trading in textiles At the outset, Ambani worked with just a chair, table and a telephone, earning a mere 4,500 rupees a month. The business had later metamorphosed into manufacturing and services.

Today, Reliance is India's largest private sector company, reporting sales of US$13.2 billion and with interests in textiles, petrochemicals, oil and gas, petroleum, financial services, insurance, telecom, media and power.

Two years ago, it set up a 27 million tonnes per annum refinery at Jamnagar in the west Indian state of Gujarat. It was the largest grassroots refinery in the world. Ambani had finally realized his oil company dream.

The seed money for some of these initial forays came from an unlikely source. Unlike other Indian businessmen who funded their operations and expansions from banks and private lenders, Ambani was the first to tap the small shareholder in a big way. Reliance set off an equity cult, the like of which has rarely been seen anywhere in the world.

The heavily-built entrepreneur always remained the favourite of stock market investors. Some of them have married, bought their first car or invested in office space by selling off part of their Reliance holdings. In 1977, the year Reliance went public, it had 58,000 shareholders. Today, the number has swelled up to 3.5 million. Long time investors have been rewarded regularly with dividends and bonuses and have seen their investments grow at a whopping 43 percent, compounded.

In the stock markets, Ambani cut a messiah-like figure. For the ordinary shareholder, he became a kind of god. Ambani focused heavily on smaller exchanges that's why the name of Reliance spread to smaller towns also. He gave investors tips on tracking shares and encouraged the habit of reading financial dailies. For the small shareholder, investing in Reliance was like converting their hard-earned money to gold.

Winning the trust of small investors and having an endless supply of cheap funds was thus a winning formula for Ambani. Another reason he succeeded in a big way was that he always thought big.

When the Birla Group, one of India's oldest business houses, made its foray into petrochemicals, it set up a 9 million tonnes per annum refinery in Karnataka state in south India. Ambani's, of course, was thrice that capacity.

For someone who did not complete schooling, the management structure in the 85,000-employee Reliance was the envy of his peers. Managers were given a free hand—but also showed the door if they failed to perform. Most of them managed to stay on and then showed an unfailing loyalty to tycoon. This saying was popular those days, "Try luring away Reliance managers even with an offer of double their salary. They will refuse; their commitment to Dhirubhai is total."

Dhirubhai with his sons & grand-children

Son of a school teacher, Ambani once said, *"I have trusted people and they have put their trust in me. I have encouraged youth, and they have never let me down. I have asked my people to take initiative and to take risks. It has paid me rich dividends. I insist on excellence. This helps us to be leaders. Reliance is built on some of these principles."*

His people's skills were legendary. He was very helpful. He followed an 'open-door' policy. Employees could walk into his cabin and discuss their problems with him. He had a special way of dealing with different groups of people, be they employees, shareholders, journalists or government officials.

Ambani's competitors alleged that he bought off officials and had legislation re-written to suit him. They recalled his earlier days and how he picked up the art of profiteering from the then-Byzantine system of controls of Indian officialdom.

He exported spices, often at a loss, and used replenishment licenses to import rayon. Later, when rayon started to be manufactured in India, he exported rayon, again at a loss, and imported nylon. Ambani was always a step ahead of the competitors. With the imported items being heavily in demand, his profit margins were rarely under 300 percent.

❏

"I believe that the success of Reliance cannot be attributed to the qualities and achievements of one individual, or even a group of individuals, but has to be viewed as a triumph of process, and a spirit that binds the entire Reliance family together."

—*Dhirubhai Ambani*

Did Not Forget
Either Friend or Foe

After the completion of his education he reached Chorwad where he lived in rented accommodation. He wanted to go to Aden in search of a job where his elder brother was employed. But he had no money to pay for his ticket and then his neighbour, helped him reach his destination.

Dhirubhai remembered that kindness even a decade later and helped the son of neighbour's daughter get a job at Reliance's Ahmedabad factory. He also helped neighbour's other relative by continuing to employ him past his retirement age.

A tourist lodge operator from Uttarakhand also remembers how he decided to drop in at the Reliance headquarters while on a visit to Mumbai. He had not seen Dhirubhai, who was once a regular client, for about two decades and was not sure if the business tycoon would place him. Dhirubhai not only remembered his old associate, he hugged him and invited him for a leisurely breakfast the next morning at Sea Wind, his multi-storeyed skyscraper residence in south Mumbai.

On the other hand, adversaries rue the day they crossed swords with the perennially smiling, seemingly rustic businessman. They include Nusli Wadia, chairman of the more than 100-year-old Bombay Dyeing textile group; Arun Shourie, the former editor of *Indian Express* who wrote scathing reports about Dhirubhai's unusual business methods; the *Mafatlals*, whose plans for expanding their petrochemicals complex on the outskirts of Mumbai were allegedly stymied by Dhirubhai's

**Dhirubhai & his sons
with Bill Clinton**

powerful 'connections' and Kapil Mehra of *Orkays*, another textiles giant, who had to face the ignominy of being locked up behind bars for a few days.

Dhirubhai, however, could not win all politicians over to his side and a former prime minister, V P Singh, had gone on a personal crusade to finish off India's most controversial businessman. There were probes by the economic offenses wing of Mumbai's crime branch, the Directorate-General of Revenue Intelligence, the Enforcement Directorate and the Income Tax Department. But inspite of all these, they emerged unscathed.

If some stock brokers helped him make the Reliance scrip the darling of investors, he destroyed those that did not. On April 30, 1982, the bears attacked, short selling the Reliance scrip and sending it plummeting from 131 rupees to 121 rupees as more than 300,000 shares hit the market. But something the bears never dreamt of happened. Challenging them, Dhirubhai's brokers bought everything that was sold. Dhirubhai then demanded delivery of the shares. The panicky bear cartel was forced to buy Reliance shares from all possible avenues. Chaos ensued and the Bombay Stock Exchange had to be closed for three days.

The Ambani reached beyond the stock markets, as Hamish McDonald, the former New Delhi bureau chief of the *Far Eastern Economic Review* and author of the unauthorized Ambani biography, *The Polyester Prince*, discovered to his dismay.

The book, brought out by an Australian publishing house, Allen & Unwin, is not kind to the Ambanis. Even though the book was published in 1998, it is still not available in Indian bookshops. That's because the Ambanis have threatened legal action for anything they perceive as defamatory in the book. And when the Ambanis say something, they really mean it.

The
Polyester
❖Prince❖

*The rise of
Dhirubhai Ambani*

Hamish McDonald

The Polyester Prince : Banned in India

Vir Sanghvi, editor of the influential *Hindustan Times* daily newspaper and a long time Ambani-watcher, has this to offer,"The answer, I suspect, is that whatever the rules of the game, Ambani will just play it so much better than the rest. If the name of the game was manipulating rules and politicians he was the champion. Now that the game involves globalization and the free market, he is still the best player in the country."

To the outside world, Dhirubhai was Reliance and Reliance was Dhirubhai. But after surviving his first stroke (February 9, 1986), which left his right hand paralyzed, and a paralytic attack two years ago, Ambani had slowly moved away from the hands-on management of the group. Of late, he had been spending only two hours a day at his office in the south Mumbai business district of Nariman Point.

The day-to-day running of the show had been left to his sons Anil, a graduate of Wharton, and Mukesh, an MBA from Standford. Anil handles marketing, corporate communications, investments and the financial markets. Mukesh is behind-the-scenes man, taking care to see that projects are executed on time. The brothers in turn delegate to a talented and devoted band of managers.

Analysts say that the group has grown quite strong over the years and has enough systems in place not to collapse overnight after its founder's demise. The organization has been fine-tuned to aptly react to any exigency or opportunity.

The thumb-rule at Reliance: Do your work with excellence? The Reliance motto: **Just Do It**.

Ambani had got it right much before Nike did it. For the shoe giant, it was only an advertising slogan. At India's largest enterprise, Ambani had perfected it into a habit.

❑

"Our dreams have to be bigger. Our ambitions higher. Our commitment deeper. And our efforts greater. This is my dream for Reliance and for India."

—Dhirubhai Ambani

Rewrote Indian Corporate History

Dhirajlal Hirachand Ambani is not just the usual rags-to-riches story. He will be remembered as the one who rewrote Indian corporate history and built a truly global corporate group.

Popularly known as Dhirubhai, the 69-year-old changed the rules of the game in the industry in an era when the private sector was hampered by the licence regime. In the process, he attracted criticism that he did not always play fair.

There is also the story of how the Ambanis blocked publication of a biography titled *The Polyester Prince* written by a foreign writer by threatening legal action for anything they perceived as defamatory in the book.

Ambani's huge success, however, dwarfed the controversies that surrounded him.

Armed with a matriculation certificate, he went to Aden only to return with a big idea of building a petroleum company.

He returned to India in 1958 with Rs 50,000 and set up a textile trading company.

Starting from scratch in 1966, Dhirubhai and his two US-educated sons—Mukesh and Anil — have built an empire that has outstripped older venerable groups like the Tatas and the Birlas.

Dhirubhai is also credited with shaping India's equity culture, attracting millions of retail investors in a market till then dominated by financial institutions.

It is fact that he built India's largest private sector company from scratch, Dhirubhai will be remembered for revolutionising capital markets. From nothing, he generated billions of rupees in wealth for those who put their trust in his companies.

Over a period of two decades, Dhirubhai's millions of investors lifted him from Rs 23 million to Rs. 600 billion.

The group flagship Reliance Industries is valued by the market at nearly Rs 300 billion, while Reliance Petroleum commands a figure of nearly Rs 170 billion. And the group's assets add up to over Rs 520 billion.

Backward and forward 'integration' became the buzzwords in the Dhirubhai group's strategy of growth. Today, the group straddles every link in the petroleum and petrochemicals value chain, beginning with oil and gas production to refining, to making intermediates and finished products like fabrics.

Dhirubhai is also credited with being the man whose efforts helped create an 'equity cult' in the Indian capital market.

With innovative instruments like the convertible debenture, Reliance quickly became a darling of the stock market in the 1980s. Today, the group has five million individual shareholders.

In 1992, Reliance became the first Indian company to raise money in global markets, its high credit-taking in international markets limited only by India's sovereign rating.

With the meteoric rise of the Ambanis came formidable power and clout. What distinguishes Reliance's growth is that much of it came not during the post-liberalisation 1990s but in the days of the 'License Raj' when there were stifling controls on the industry.

Dhirubhai managed to get his way and created his empire with remarkable ease, a way his business rivals could not digest easily. They accuse the group of subverting the system in its penchant for growth.

Critics accuse the group of resorting to all tricks of the trade and breaking all rules of the game. The corridors of power in Delhi and elsewhere are replete with stories of what the Dhirubhai influence could do to the careers of politicians and bureaucrats.

Every Cabinet and bureaucratic reshuffle spurred a string of such stories. But the Ambanis were not bothered about these reports and ascribe such writings to the campaign by rivals inspired by jealousy.

While the Ambanis inspire admiration and serve as role models, they are also controversial. Back in the mid-1980s, stories used to do rounds of their clout in the power corridor when they were locked in a bitter spat with Bombay Dyeing's Nusli Wadia. The Reliance group is also often the target of campaign by adversaries.

In his relentless run to the pinnacle, Dhirubhai became the highest-paid chief executive officer with a salary of Rs 88.5 million leaving Wipro's Azim Premji far behind at Rs 42 million. Both are among the world's top 500 billionaires.

❑

"There is no question about that (retirement). Business is my hobby. It is not a burden to me. In any case, Reliance now can run without me."

—Dhirubhai Ambani

'My Success is My Worst Enemy'

The meteoric rise of Ambani and his challenge to established business houses made him an obvious target for detractors, all the more since he was a complete outsider, relying on his wits instead of family connections to make his fortune.

His vaulting ambition, his appetite for risk and his swashbuckling larger-than-life image made him a natural target for those who resented his meteoric rise to the top of the business ladder. He wasn't just the veteran of many battles—his whole life was one big battle.

Throttling the bears

In March 1982, the Reliance scrip was the target of a bear raid organised by a Kolkata based industrialist. They picked the wrong target.

While the share was being hammered down by the bears, Dhirubhai organised a rescue operation, with friendly brokers buying up every share being sold. Then, knowing fully well that the brokers did not have possession of the shares they had sold, he demanded delivery.

The bear cartel was thrown into a panic and desperately started buying Reliance shares. When cartel members asked for time to deliver the shares, Dhirubhai asked his friends to refuse. The upshot - the Bombay Stock Exchange had to be shut for three days. But the bears had been taught a lesson - do not meddle in Reliance shares.

It wasn't long, however, before Dhirubhai's enemies raised a simple question -where did he, till recently a yarn trader and only a budding industrialist, get hold of the money needed to stop the bears in their tracks?

The answer was delivered by the then Finance Minister who announced in Parliament that non-resident Indians had invested over Rs 220 million in Reliance during 1982-83. These investments had also been made by companies with names like Crocodile, Lota and Fiasco.

Investigations by journalists revealed that these companies had been registered in the Isle of Man, the tax haven, by several people sporting the surname *Shah*. Who did these companies belong to? Questions were raised and fingers pointed, but a Reserve Bank of India enquiry could not find any wrong doing by Reliance.

The matter died a natural death.

The debenture issues

Dhirubhai had always understood finance very well, amply illustrated by the fact that Reliance paid virtually zero tax. In 1984, a cash-strapped Dhirubhai hit upon a brainwave.

Reliance had issued plenty of non-convertible debentures, and his standing among investors was God-like. Why not, he reasoned, convert the debentures into equity? That would improve the company's debt equity ratio, reduce outflow on interest, and allow him to raise funds once again.

The trouble was that these debentures were non-convertible. But Dhirubhai was not the one to let a little thing like that stands in his way. He managed to convince the finance ministry and investors lapped up his offer.

Unfortunately, V P Singh was not so easily convinced. A day before the Reliance board was to meet to consider another round of conversions in June 1986, V P Singh refused to permit it. All hell broke loose, with Reliance's debenture prices halving within a matter of hours.

That was not the end of the affair. Banks had lent heavily against the security of Reliance shares to about 60 investment companies, which were buying Reliance debentures. The *Indian Express* alleged that these companies were fronting for Reliance, and the whole operation made sense only if the debentures could be converted to shares.

The revelations led to an almighty stink, and, with the conversion not going through, the RBI ordered the banks to call back the loans. The entire episode took a heavy toll on Dhirubhai's health, and he suffered a paralytic stroke on February 9, 1986.

In December 1986, in a move dubbed as a referendum on Reliance by the media, a Rs 5 billion convertible debenture issue by Reliance was oversubscribed seven times.

Soon after, VP Singh was shifted from the finance ministry. The early conversion of the debentures into shares was permitted. Pending licences were cleared.

The one battle lost

One corporate battle which Dhirubhai did not win was the battle for control of Larsen & Toubro. In 1988, L&T was in bad shape, and the Ambanis thought that the time was ripe for an acquisition. Having secured the support of L&T's chairman, who saw Dhirubhai as a white knight in the battle against the raider Manu Chhabria, Mukesh and Anil Ambani became directors of L&T. By April 1989, Dhirubhai became chairman of L&T.

Unfortunately, things didn't go smoothly. In December Reliance's old bete noire, VP Singh, became prime minister. The *Indian Express* once again did the muck-raking, and found that the takeover had been effected by financial institutions like the Life Insurance Corporation and the General Insurance Corporation selling their shares. Since the institutions were not allowed to sell to private parties, the *Indian Express* alleged that the whole operation was a fraud.

The matter moved to the courts. Sensing defeat, the Ambanis reversed the transaction, taking a substantial loss. An extraordinary general meeting was called to decide whether the Ambanis would remain on the L&T board. Dhirubhai resigned. Eleven years later, Reliance sold its holdings in L&T to Grasim. Even that transaction was not free of controversy, as the Securities and Exchange Board of India felt that Reliance should not have bought L&T shares from the market a few months before deciding to sell its stake. The insider trading charge was settled with Reliance paying a nominal fine.

The share switch-hitch

Another battle was the share switch controversy. Here too Dhirubhai did not come off all that well. Apparently, when Unit Trust of India sent some Reliance shares to its registrars for transfer, it received some other shares —with different numbers —in return.

The markets jumped to the conclusion that there was something fishy—perhaps even fake shares in play. SEBI's investigation into the matter did not find evidence of this, but there were lots of discrepancies in the numbering of shares issued and the share transfer process was found to have many loopholes.

For a man who single-handedly created the equity cult, Dhirubhai was seen as running a less-than-tidy ship in its share transfer operations. Sebi asked Reliance Consultancy Services, the group's registrar, to shut shop. And the crisis blew over.

In the wireless loop

Reliance also attracted controversy when the telecom sector was being opened up. Initial regulation of the sector involved clear-cut lines of demarcation between cellular and basic operators.

At the same time, wireless in local loop technology offered the possibility of limited mobility. WLL supporters pointed to its cheapness and called it limited mobility for the masses.

Cellular operators, on the other hand, protested that limited mobility was an infringement on their turf, and unjustified because they had paid hefty licence fees. Reliance critics lost no time in pointing out that since the Reliance group held basic licences in many telecom circles, they would be one of the principal beneficiaries if basic operators were allowed entry to the limited mobility segment.

The telecom regulator, however, did allow limited mobility, albeit with restrictions limiting the area in which it could be used. The matter continues to be dogged by controversy, with the parties taking recourse to the courts. There have been other battles and controversies, the most recent one being the alleged infringement of the Official Secrets Act by Reliance employees.

Dhirubhai's position as an outsider in India's business world meant that he has had to deal with more than the normal share of jealousy and animosity. But that did not dim his zest for battle or derail his dream of making Reliance the largest private sector company in India.

❑

"Give the youth a proper environment. Motivate them. Extend them the support they need. Each one of them has infinite source of energy. They will deliver."

—Dhirubhai Ambani

END OF AN ERA

Reliance: When Dhirubhai Died

The 69-year-old Ambani was widely acclaimed as the father of India's stock market culture. He broke the monopoly of banks as the source of corporate financing by raising tens of millions of dollars from retail investors.

The company he founded, petrochemicals major Reliance Industries, made an initial public offering in 1977 at a time when retail investors shunned stock markets. Today Reliance has over 3.5 million shareholders, making it one of the most widely held stocks in the world.

The combined sales of the Reliance group, which has interests ranging from petrochemicals and oil to telecommunications and power, account for nearly three per cent of India's gross domestic product.

The aggregate market value of the four listed companies in the Reliance conglomerate is about $9 billion.

Reliance Petroleum, which operates the world's largest grassroots refinery, Reliance Industrial Infrastructure, an engineering firm, and financial services provider Reliance Capital are the other publicly listed companies.

The Reliance group owns a 64 per cent stake in Reliance Petroleum, a 26 per cent stake in unlisted Reliance Telecom and 45 per cent of Reliance Infocom, which is also not listed. Reliance Infocom is the umbrella company for the group's expansion into telecom and information technology. Reliance Telecom has licences for providing basic and cellular telecom services.

Reliance Telecom has operations in 86 towns and a subscriber base of 187,000 users. Reliance Infocom is building a network connecting 115 cities via a 60,000-km (37,280 mile) fibre optic cable backbone.

The following are key facts and statistics on the Reliance group as on March 31, 2002.

- Aggregate turnover: Rs 600 billion ($12.3 billion).
- Net profit: Rs 46 billion.
- Total assets: Rs 550 billion.

Assets of Reliance Industries

- 25 offshore and onshore oil and gas exploration and production blocks, covering an area of 175,000 sq km.
- World's largest paraxylene plant at 1.4 million tonnes per year, making Reliance the world's third-largest producer.
- World's fourth-largest purified terephthalic acid maker with capacity of more than one million tonnes per year.
- World's sixth-largest polypropylene capacity of one million tonnes per year.
- A 26 per cent shareholding in Reliance Telecom which offers basic and cellular services to an area covering one third of the country and a third of India's one billion-plus population.
- A 45 per cent stake in Reliance Infocom, which is spending $5 billion to set up a nationwide broadband telecommunications network to offer the whole range of voice and data services.

The Reliance group owns

- A 27 per cent holding in power utility BSES Ltd.
- A 30 per cent stake in an oil and gas exploration joint venture with state-run Oil and Natural Gas Corporation and tl.e BG Group.

- A 64 per cent stake in Reliance Petroleum, the fifth-largest refinery in the world with the capacity to produce 27 million tonnes per year of petroleum products.

Shareholding Profile

- RIL has over 3.5 million shareholders.
- In Reliance Industries, the Ambanis own a 44 per cent stake, institutional investors own 32 per cent and the remaining 24 per cent is owned by other shareholders.
- Reliance group owns 64 per cent in Reliance Petroleum, institutional investors own 13 per cent and other shareholders 23 per cent.

❏

"Always be the silent benefactor. Don't tom-tom about how you helped someone."

–Dhirubhai Ambani

Mere Dream: India,
A Super Power

Reliance group Chairman Dhirubhai Ambani, one of the leading lights of the Indian corporate world, was confident that India will become a superpower one day.

Following are his famous quotes during interviews with various publications and public speeches:

- "We can prove to the world that India can do it. That Indians are not afraid of competition. That India is a nation of achievers."

- "I dream India of becoming a great economic superpower."

- "Dhirubhai will go one day. But Reliance's employees and shareholders will keep it afloat. Reliance is now a concept in which the Ambanis have become irrelevant."

- "Reliance is built on some principles. I sincerely believe that these are the principles that can help us to build a greater India."

- "We must forge a new partnership for a great India. A strong and constructive partnership between industry, government and society."

- "Pursue your goal, even in the face of difficulties. Convert difficulties into opportunities. Keep your morale high, in spite of setbacks. At the end, you are bound to succeed."

- "If India wants to be a great nation, we must have courage to trust. This is my sincere belief."

- "We must always go for the best. Do not compromise on

quality. Reject if it is not the best — not only the best in India, but globally."

- On his retirement: "There is no question about that. Business is my hobby. It is not a burden to me. In any case, Reliance now can run without me." He made these observations in 1994.

- "I give least importance to being Number one. I consider myself to be fortunate in this position and would like to contribute to nation building in some way."

- "I am in favour of 100 per cent pro-liberalisation. I do not think any industrialist is against it. But we should protect our industries, from unfair competition."

- Does making money excite you? "No, but I have to make money for my shareholders. What excites me is achievement, doing something difficult. In this room, extraordinary things must happen."

- "All we have to do is to break the shackles that chain the energies of our people, and India's economy will record a quantum leap and move into a new, higher orbit of growth, competitiveness and productivity."

- "First and foremost, I owe my success and achievements to the affection, friendship and trust of millions of employees, customers, shareholders, and business associates, who have stood by me and been a major source of my strength all along."

- "I believe that the success of Reliance cannot be attributed to the qualities and achievements of one individual, or even a group of individuals, but has to be viewed as a triumph of process, and a spirit that binds the entire Reliance family together."

- "My advice to young entrepreneurs is not to accept defeat in the face of odds, and challenge negative forces with hope, self-confidence and conviction. I believe that ambition and initiative will ultimately triumph. The success of the young entrepreneur will be the key to India's transformation in the new millennium."

● "I can never fully repay the debt I owe to Mumbai. My past was shaped in Mumbai."

● "I consider myself a pathfinder. I have been excavating the jungle and making the road for others to walk. I like to be the first in everything I do."

● "I as school kid was a member of the Civil Guard, something like today's NCC. We had to salute our officers who went round in jeeps. So I thought...one day I will also ride in a jeep and somebody else will salute me."

● "Growth has no limit in Reliance. I keep revising my vision. A vision has to be within reach, not in the air. It has to be achievable. I believe we can be a Rs 300 billion company by the end of the century."

● "My fulfillment lies in the satisfaction of every member of the Reliance family, comprising thousands of workers, managers, business associates and over five million shareholders. Being instrumental in creating wealth for over 5 million Indian families, and bringing prosperity and well being to their life is the best source of satisfaction and joy for me."

❑

"True entrepreneurship comes only from risk-taking."
                                        —Dhirubhai Ambani

The End of an Era

Never before had an industrialist's death brought such a crowd at the funeral. But then Dhirajlal Hirachand Ambani, Dhirubhai to all, was no mere industrialist.

Indeed, the collective stream of visitors had begun with the news of his hospitalisation. Mumbai's Breach Candy Hospital had become a gathering ground of the who's who of the country. Politicians, industrialists, film stars—it seemed as if there were no one whose life Dhirubhai would not have touched.

The trust and faith in the man was almost infinite. Stories about his humility, power and reach are the stuff of urban legends.

A businessman who had known him closely summed it up best, "If the doctors can just get him back to his senses, Dhirubhai will pull through. We have faith in his willpower."

But it was not to be. The man who wouldn't ever give up, finally went down fighting the grim battle for survival for 13 days at the Breach Candy hospital in Mumbai. Dhirubhai's body was brought to his residence, Sea Wind, at Cuffe Parade in south-Mumbai where it was kept for last respects while children Mukesh, Anil, Nina and Dipti and daughters-in-law Neeta and Tina stood by.

And thousands turned up to pay their respects in one never-ending stream of visitors, covering the full spectrum of society. From the leaders of India Inc to the stars of bollywood, from politicians and senior bureaucrats to shareholders and employees. It was a veritable who's who of India, from Ratan Tata to Amitabh Bachchan to Bal Thackeray. From emissaries from the prime minister to the leader of opposition. All the ministers and chief ministers cutting across party lines came to pay their tributes.

By afternoon people were asked to leave the premises so that arrangements could be made to take the body for cremation, but outside the crowds just swelled, pleading with the security guards to allow them in.

The body was taken to Marine Lines in an open truck with sons and family members and associates standing beside brothers Mukesh and Anil. But the streets were packed with thousands of people — on trees, on the foot-overbridge, even on electric poles. For the last 15 metres, Dhirubhai's body was carried on his sons' shoulders.

"Dhirubhaiji amar rahe (Long live Dhirubhai)" screamed the crowd as many lunged towards the body, just to touch it, in the hope perhaps that his Midas touch would rub off on them, struggling towards his body, braving police lathis.

Many of these may have been those who had become billionaires by merely buying his company's shares at the right time. But there were many to whom he was an idol to be emulated. A real story in a city that sells tinsel dreams of rags to riches.

"Dhirubhai will go one day," he had said in an interview long back, *"but Reliance's employees and shareholders will keep it afloat. Reliance is now a concept in which the Ambanis have become irrelevant."*

Earlier, the body was kept at the basement of his residence, 'Sea Wind' to enable friends, admirers, shareholders, politicians and industry leaders to pay their last respects. The then Minister of State in the Prime Minister's Office, Vijay Goel, placed a wreath on the body of the deceased industrialist on behalf of the then Prime Minister, Atal Behari Vajpayee. Goel said that his life would be known as a success story of a person who never forgot his past despite reaching towering heights.

The then Deputy Prime Minister, L.K. Advani, flew to Mumbai, cutting short his Gujarat tour and said Ambani was the embodiment of initiative, enterprise and determination. "He was one of the greatest achievers in the country and would remain an inspiration for others."

Among the dignitaries who came to pay their last respects were the former prime minister, Deve Gowda, the Gujarat Chief Minister, Narendra Modi, the then Minister of State for Tourism, Vinod Khanna, the Samajwadi Party leaders, Mulayam Singh Yadav, Amar Singh, the Shiv Sena chief, Balasaheb Thackeray, the Nationalist Congress Party leader, Sharad Pawar, industrialists, Ratan Tata, M.S. Banga, Adi Godrej, MPs Praful Patel, Shabana Azmi and Murli Deora. Also among the visitors were film stars Amitabh Bachchan, Dilip Kumar and other celebrities from the film and media world.

Mukesh and Anil Ambani, his sons who have largely been responsible for Reliance's meteoric rise since Dhirubhai's first stroke in the 80s, have not become irrelevant, but Dhirubhai does leave behind a concept that has captured the imagination of many an entrepreneur can do.

❑

"If India wants to be a great nation, we must have courage to trust. This is my sincere belief."

—*Dhirubhai Ambani*

Rich Tributes

It was clearly the most overwhelming reaction from the political world over the death of a business tycoon: President KR Narayanan, Vice President Krishan Kant, Prime Minister Atal Bihari Vajpayee, Deputy Prime Minister L.K. Advani and Congress President Sonia Gandhi led scores of cabinet ministers, chief ministers and other political leaders in paying tributes to Dhirubhai Ambani.

Mr Vajpayee said, "The country has lost an iconic proof of what an ordinary Indian fired by the spirit of enterprise and driven by determination, can achieve in his own lifetime", adding that he was "filled with profound grief at the demise of Dhirubhai Ambani".

Minister of State in the Prime Minister's Office, **Vijay Goel** represented Mr Vajpayee at the funeral.

Mr Narayanan said, "Mr Ambani's emergence as a leading figure in the corporate world is a remarkable example, which needs to be studied in depth to highlight his important role in India's quest for economic growth and re-generation."

Vice-President **Krishan Kant** said, "Mr Ambani was one of the principal architects of India's entrepreneurial renaissance."

Deputy Prime Minister **L.K. Advani** said he was an example for other industrialists and businessmen of the country in the present era of stiff competition.

Finance minister **Jaswant Singh** said Mr Ambani's life epitomises the spirit of entrepreneurship and unflagging demonstration which in human history has created an enduring institution.

Lok Sabha Speaker **Manohar Joshi** described Mr Ambani as a shining star on the industrial map of India.

Bharatiya Janata Party president **M Venkaiah Naidu** said Mr Ambani created an industrial empire which immensely added to the economic growth of the country.

Congress President **Sonia Gandhi** also condoled the death and deputed former Union Minister **R.K. Dhawan** to pay respects to the departed soul.

According to leader of the Opposition in the Rajya Sabha and former finance minister **Dr Manmohan Singh**, Mr Ambani was the "greatest captain of Indian industry in recent times...A great visionary, innovator and an entrepreneur of extraordinary abilities".

Describing Mr Ambani as a pioneer, Samajwadi Party President **Mulayam Singh Yadav** said that the rise from a boy in a poor family to the biggest industrialist of the country is a lesson to the people that anything can be achieved if a person honestly and dedicatedly worked for it.

Uttaranchal (now Uttarakhand) chief minister **N.D. Tiwari** said: "From an ordinary man, he rose to be an industrial giant, providing inspiration to thousands of people. His life is a lesson in will power and hard work."

Bihar chief minister **Rabri Devi** and Rashtriya Janata Dal supremo **Laloo Prasad Yadav** also condoled Mr Ambani's death.

❏

"Dhirubhai will go one day. But Reliance's employees and shareholders will keep it afloat. Reliance is now a concept in which the Ambanis have become irrelevant."

–Dhirubhai Ambani

Reliance Group
Break-up Saga

On June 18, 2005, Kokilaben Ambani, wife of Late Dhirubhai Ambani—the founder of Reliance Group, announced that the dispute relating to the division of Rs. 1000 billion Reliance Group had been amicably settled.

She announced that the elder son Mukesh would have the 'responsibility' for Reliance Industries (RIL) and IPCL, while

Failed to abridge differences

the younger son Anil would have the 'responsibility' for Reliance Infocom, Reliance Energy and Reliance Capital.

With this announcement, the dispute with charges and counter-charges between the brothers, Mukesh and Anil came to an end. The settlement was expected by many to bring about more transparency and professionalism in the

Reliance Group. The shareholders of the Group, the Indian government and the stock markets reacted positively to the resolution of the dispute.

In a span of three decades, RIL, the flagship company of the Reliance Group, had come a long way—from a synthetic yarn trader, to the only private company in India figuring in the Fortune 500 list.

Reliance Group was the largest industrial house in India in 2004 with total group sales of Rs. 900 billion.

Reliance had over 80,000 employees, accounted for 3% of India's GDP and 9% of all indirect tax revenues paid to the Government of India.

Battle of Billionaire Brothers

India's billionaire Ambani brothers are at loggerheads again— this time over a rich gas field—and the row has taken a political twist with the government intervening in the bitter dispute.

At stake is the price at which tycoon Mukesh Ambani's Reliance Industries Ltd (RIL) will sell gas from an offshore block in the vast Krishna-Godavari basin to a company owned by his younger brother Anil Ambani.

The seeds of the latest battle between two of India's biggest corporate names lie in a deal carving up the Reliance empire after the 2002 death of their father Dhirubhai Ambani, who left no will.

In that family pact in 2005, Mukesh agreed to sell 28-million cubic meters of gas per day

A working site at Krishna-Godavari Basin

to his brother's company Reliance Natural Resources Ltd (RNRL) at \$2.34 per million British thermal unit (mBtu) for 17 years.

Later, Mukesh's Reliance Industries Ltd, India's largest private company, sought to change the sale price.

Fossil fuel fight

It cited a 2007 government order which said gas from the field, one of Asia's largest fossil fuel finds, can't be sold below \$4.20 per mBtu—44 percent higher than the price set out in the brothers' pact.

Anil, who wants a part of the gas for his group's power plants, won a ruling from the Bombay High Court saying the pact should be upheld.

But now the case is before the Supreme Court and the government, which controls fuel prices, has stepped in, insisting the supply agreement cancelled.

The government has asked the court to annul the deal on grounds the siblings cannot set a price for the gas, a

In the court—unable to settle the dispute themselves

scarce resource in energy-hungry India.

Government cannot leave the industrial development of the country at their mercy and have contractors of gas fields decide on their own on the utilisation and price of gas.

Unlawful design

But in a court affidavit, Anil's firm accused the government of 'blatantly and openly supporting' RIL's 'unlawful design' to wriggle out of its commitment.

Anil appealed to Premier Manmohan Singh to stop the oil ministry from 'overtly and covertly' intervening in the row with his brother's company, which he accuses of 'corporate greed'.

The government said it is acting in the national interest, calling the 'private agreement' a threat to the country's industrial development.

Mukesh's RIL had said that the agreement between the brothers stipulated that "the supply of gas was subject to availability and approval by the Government."

The row is the latest in a series of many high pitched battles between the brothers.

They went head-to-head last year over a blockbuster merger deal being negotiated by Anil with South African telecom giant MTN to create an emerging-market telecoms behemoth.

Those talks hit the rocks after Mukesh told MTN that he had first right of refusal to buy a controlling stake in Anil's flagship Reliance Communications.

The brothers appeared to work well together when their father was alive but relations soured after they inherited the oil-to-communications empire.

The discord between Mukesh and Anil came to a head in 2004 after Mukesh had the RIL board pass a motion telling all directors, including Anil, to report to him, saying it was his father's wish.

Split Chronology

- **2004**
  - ❖ *Nov, 18:* Mukesh Ambani admits to ownership issues in Reliance.
  - ❖ *Nov 22:* Anil asks mother Kokilaben to settle the issue.
  - ❖ *Nov 23:* Mukesh's shots off e-mail to RIL employees stating that CMD is the final authority. Independent director M L Bhakta quits.

- ❖ Reports say RIL Board bestowed overwhelming powers to Mukesh in a meet held on July 27, 2004, triggering tension between the Ambani brothers.
- ❖ *Nov 25:* Six directors quit Reliance Energy (REL).
- ❖ *Nov 29:* Anil's letter to REL staff.
- ❖ *Nov 30:* REL board asks directors who quit to reconsider their decision
- ❖ *Dec 2:* RIL's Rs 8,100 crore investment in Reliance Infocom comes to the fore.
- ❖ *Dec 8:* Reports say Mukesh got 12% equity in Infocomm.
- ❖ *Dec 12:* REL seeks RIL's opinion on gas supply
- ❖ *Dec 13:* Market regulator SEBI asks bourses to look into RIL corporate governance issues.
- ❖ *Dec15:* Anil seeks board meeting to discuss corporate governance issues.
- ❖ *Dec 20:* Anil aide Amitabh Juhunjhunwala quits as RIL treasurer and REL director.
- ❖ *Dec 23:* Mukesh gives up 50 crore sweat equity in Reliance Infocomm

- **2005**
- ❖ *Jan 3:* Anil quits IPCL board, blasts Mukesh aide Anand Jain.
- ❖ *Jan 19:* REL directors withdraw resignation.
- ❖ *Jan21:* Reliance board backs Mukesh on buyback, ignores Anil's pleas on corporate governance issues
- ❖ *Feb 15:* Infocom takes back one crore shares gifted to Ashish Deora
- ❖ *Mar 9:* ICICI 's K V Kamat completes Reliance valuation
- ❖ *April 7:* Anil alleges phone tapping.
- ❖ *April 27:* Anil refuses to sign RIL accounts for 2004-05.
- ❖ *June 18:* Kokilaben announces Reliance settlement.

❑

HONOURS & ACCOLADES

Wharton Dean's Medal for Dhirubhai

Reliance Industries Limited Chairman Dhirajlal Hirachand Ambani became the 24th person and the first Indian to be awarded the Wharton School Dean's Medal.

At a glittering ceremony in Mumbai, politicians, business-persons, the Reliance staff, and a huge media corps turned out to felicitate the chairman of India's largest private sector company, Reliance Industries Limited.

In his acceptance speech, Dhirubhai said that he accepted the award in humility and on behalf of the Ambani family comprising his immediate family, the staff of Reliance, the dealers and associates, and his investors.

A galaxy of politicians and entrepreneurs attended the ceremony

He said that even as he spoke, 80,000 workers were toiling away in Jamnagar, Gujarat, which was devastated in the recent cyclone, to repair the damage to the Reliance petrol refinery in record time and he was proud of them.

Ambani said while he was satisfied at having created wealth for over 5 million shareholders, he added that it was not enough and that wealth needed to be created for 500 million people.

"Our dreams have to be bigger, ambitions higher, commitment deeper and efforts greater. This is my dream for Reliance. It is my dream for India," he said.

Ambani said that he was inspired by the determination of American pioneers, who laid the foundation of the world's richest nation. "They gave respect to the creation of wealth," he said, adding that the Indian ethos was no different.

He said that on the occasion of Diwali, Indians worship the goddess Laxmi, but the meaning of this ceremony was lost along with the country's freedom. Bureaucracy became the most respected institution, and even after Independence, the mindset remained the same, he stated.

However, he added that big changes are taking place and this evening was a proof of the same.

To the youth, he advised them not to accept defeat and to challenge the negative forces, and they would certainly win. "You will succeed because India is no longer in the feudal age," he declared.

The award winner pointed that performance matters much in today's context. He urged greater speed in making India an economic superpower in the next 25 years.

Presenting the medal, Dean Thomas Gerrity of the Wharton School, University of Pennsylvania, United States, said that the award was in recognition of Dhirubhai Ambani's entrepreneurial ability and to recognise the triumph of the human spirit.

Gerrity pointed out that Dhirubhai had created world standards at a time when the Indian economy was not much strong and most other industrialists were only too pleased to operate in a protected environment.

He said that when Reliance had difficulty in finding funds for business, Ambani had gone to the people and sought the funds of investors. The first Reliance public issue in 1977 had 58,000 investors; today there are four million equity holders!

Reliance, he said, was responsible more than any other in creating an equity culture in India. Moreover, it had always rewarded the investors well, at an average of 30 per cent dividend, when such was not the fashion.

Today, said Gerrity, Reliance is a global company, and it is building the world's largest grassroot refinery at Jamnagar. All this is from a businessman who started his operations from one small room in Mumbai and lived in a one-room tenement with his wife, four children, and two more relatives.

Tracing the incredible Dhirubhai saga, the dean reminded the audience that, unlike many other industrialists today, Dhirubhai boasted no pedigree. He was the third of five children of a school teacher in Chorwad, a village in Gujarat. The recipient of an award from the world's leading business school could not afford university education!

Gerrity recalled that Dhirubhai started his career at the age of 17, when he went to work in Aden in 1958. "He started as an attendant at Shell Petroleum, and soon learnt everything in the business. He became the manager and it was here that for the first time he dreamt big."

The Wharton Dean told the audience that on his return to India, Dhirubhai began trading in textiles and commodities in 1966. "At one time, Dhirubhai sold dirt to an Arab sheikh who wanted to grow roses in the desert," said the dean. From a trader, Dhirubhai began his great process of backward integration. "He saw the rising demand for polyester, and set up his first mill in 1966 with an investment of just Rs 2.7 million," said Gerrity.

He pointed out that Dhirubhai was a great believer in modern technology and fully trained workers. "In 1975, a World

Bank team concluded that only the Reliance factories would be acceptable in the developed countries," he said.

Also speaking at the ceremony, the then finance minister Palaniappan Chidambaram said that Dhirubhai's achievements are a triumph of vision over an inward-looking habit and a triumph of faith and confidence over criticism.

He pointed out that Dhirubhai had gone to create wealth when doing so was considered a lowly profession. Chidambaram added that he saluted Dhirubhai for choosing not to become a non-resident Indian.

The then Maharashtra Chief Minister Manohar Joshi — tongue firmly in cheek — said that all school teachers or sons of school teachers achieve greatness. Joshi, incidentally, is also a teacher and runs his own private classes.

The thenMadhya Pradesh Chief Minister Digvijay Singh said before he felicitated Dhirubhai, he would salute his wife, Kokilaben Ambani, for the support she gave to her husband.

❑

"Money is not a product by itself, it is a by-product, so don't chase it."

—Dhirubhai Ambani

Wharton School
Honours Dhirubhai

The Wharton School of the University of Pennsylvania has named a 300-seat, state-of-the-art auditorium as the Dhirubhai Ambani Auditorium in honour of the late founder chairman of Reliance Industries Ltd.

The naming was announced at a special dedication ceremony in Philadelphia with a multi-million dollar gift from his son, Anil Dhirubhai Ambani, chairman of Reliance Anil Dhirubhai Ambani Group.

"We are deeply grateful for this outstanding gift and are proud to name this prominent facility for Dhirubhai Ambani," said Wharton Dean Patrick Harker as several members of the Ambani family, including Dhirubhai Ambani's wife Kokilaben and Anil Ambani's wife Tina Ambani joined Wharton School administrators at the ribbon-cutting ceremony.

"He was a true pioneer in the development of the Indian economy, opening opportunity to thousands of his fellow citizens through his then-innovative public stock offerings. We are honoured to have this outstanding opportunity to pay last tribute to Mr Ambani and the companies he built, and the important role he played in India's economic growth, and we are grateful to his son Anil for choosing to remember him in this meaningful way," Harker said.

Dhirubhai Ambani was awarded the prestigious Dean's Medal from the Wharton School in 1998.

As the 24th recipient of this honour, Ambani was recognized for his work as chairman of Reliance Industries Limited, and for his role in revolutionizing the concept of investing in India through the creation of wealth and value for millions of shareholders.

Anil Ambani received his MBA from Wharton in 1983 and currently serves as a member of the Board of Overseers.

Founded in 1881 as the first collegiate business school, The Wharton School is recognised globally for intellectual leadership and ongoing innovation across every major discipline of business education.

The school has more than 4,600 undergraduates, MBAs, executive MBA, and doctoral students; more than 8,000 annual participants in executive education programs; and an alumni network of more than 81,000 graduates.

Reliance Anil Dhirubhai Ambani Group is one of India's leading private sector organisations, with a global customer base of over 50 million. The interests of the group range from communications and financial services, to generation, transmission and distribution of power, infrastructure and entertainment. Its shareholder base of over 8 million is among the largest in the world.

❑

> "Dream big, but dream with your eyes open."
> —Dhirubhai Ambani

INHERITED
RICH LEGACY

Mukesh Ambani

Born to Dhirubhai and Kokilaben Ambani on 19 April, 1957 in Aden (Yaman) Mukesh Ambani is the chairman and managing director of Reliance Industries Limited, India's largest private sector company.

Mukesh Ambani is a Chemical Engineer from University Institute of Chemical Technology, University of Mumbai (earlier University of Bombay). He has pursued MBA from Stanford University, USA.

Mukesh, son of Dhirubhai H. Ambani, Founder Chairman of the Company joined Reliance in 1981. He initiated Reliance's backward integration journey from textiles into polyester fibres and further into petrochemicals, petroleum refining and going up-stream into oil and gas exploration and production. He created several new world class manufacturing facilities involving diverse technologies that have raised Reliance's petrochemicals manufacturing capacities from less than a million tonnes to about twenty million tonnes per year.

Working hands-on, Mukesh Ambani led the creation of the world's largest grassroots petroleum refinery at Jamnagar, India, with a current capacity of 660,000 barrels per day (33 million tonnes per year) integrated with petrochemicals, power generation, port and related infrastructures. Further, he steered the setting up of another 27 million tonnes refinery next to the existing one in Jamnagar. An aggregate refining capacity of 1.24 million barrels of oil per day has transformed "Jamnagar" as the 'Refining Hub of the World'.

In September 2008, when the first drop of crude oil flowed from the Krishna-Godavari basin, Mukesh Ambani's vision of energy security for India was being realized. Under his leadership, RIL is set to transform India's energy landscape from the oil & gas flowing from Dhirubhai 1 & 3 Natural gas —a low carbon, low polluting green fuel that will flow from these and will create value and be beneficial to a large section of India's society.

Mukesh Ambani has set up one of the largest

Mukesh with his family

and most complex information and communications technology initiative in the world in the form of Reliance Infocomm Limited (now Reliance Communications Limited).

Mukesh Ambani is also steering Reliance's development of infrastructure facilities and implementation of a pan-India organized retail network spanning multiple formats and supply chain infrastructure.

Achievements & Citations

Mukesh Ambani's achievements have been acknowledged at national and international levels. Over the years, some of the awards and recognition bestowed on him are :

- Conferred the 'Indian Corporate Citizen of the Year' by the India Leadership conclave 2009.
- Bestowed the US-India Business Council (USIBC) 'Global Vision' 2007 Award for Leadership in 2007.
- Conferred 'ET Business Leader of the Year' Award by The Economic Times (India) in the year 2006.
- Conferred the Degree Honoris Causa, Honorary Doctorate by the Maharaja Sayajirao University in 2007.
- Conferred the India Business Leadership Award by CNBC-TV18 in 2007.
- Received the first NDTV-Profit 'Global Indian Leader Award' from Hon'ble Prime Minister of India, Shri Manmohan Singh in New Delhi in the year 2006.
- Had the distinction and honour of being the Co-chair at the World Economic Forum in Davos, Switzerland in 2006.
- Ranked 42nd among the 'World's Most Respected Business Leaders' and second among the four Indian CEOs featured in a survey conducted by Pricewaterhouse Coopers and published in Financial Times, London, in 2004.
- Conferred the World Communication Award for the 'Most

Influential Person' in Telecommunications by Total Telecom, in 2004.

- Conferred the 'Asia Society Leadership Award' by the Asia Society, Washington D.C., USA, in 2004.

Mukesh Ambani is a member of the Prime Minister's Council on Trade and Industry, Government of India and the Board of Governors of the National Council of Applied Economic Research, New Delhi.

On invitation to Mukesh Ambani, Reliance Industries Limited, became a Council Member of World Business Council for Sustainable Development (WBCSD) in 2007. Mukesh Ambani has been elected as Vice Chairman of WBCSD Executive Committee in 2008.

Further, he is a member of the Indo-US CEOs Forum, the International Advisory Board of Citigroup, International Advisory Board of the National Board of Kuwait, Advisory Council for the Graduate School of Business, Stanford University, International Advisory Board of Brookings, International Advisory Board of Council on Foreign Relations, Member of The Business Council, and McKinsey Knowledge Advisory Council.

He is the Chairman, Board of Governors of the Indian Institute of Management, Bangalore, Chairman of Pandit

The Jamnagar Refinery

Deendayal Petroleum University, Gandhinagar, Co-Chair of India-Russia CEO Council, Co-Chair of Japan-India Business Leader's Forum and a member of the Advisory Council of the Indian Institute of Technology, Mumbai.

Mukesh Ambani is also the Chairman of Reliance Retail Limited and the Director of Reliance Europe Limited.

At RIL, Mukesh Ambani is the Chairman of the Finance Committee and the Employees Stock Compensation Committee.

❏

"*I give least importance to being Number one. I consider myself to be fortunate in this position and would like to contribute to nation building in some way.*"

—Dhirubhai Ambani

Reliance Industries

The Reliance Group founded by Dhirubhai H. Ambani is India's largest private sector enterprise. Reliance Industries is a Fortune Global 500 company. The Reliance Industries formally spilt on 18 June, 2005 under the patronage of Kokilaben, mother of Mukesh and Anil.

The primary business of the company is petroleum refining and petrochemicals. The company also deals in retail trading. It operates a 33 million tonnes refinery at Jamnagar in the Indian state of Gujarat. Reliance has also completed a second refinery of 29 million tons at the same site which started operations in December 2008. The company is also involved in oil & gas exploration and production. In 2002, it struck a major find on India's eastern coast in the KGB (Krishna Godavari Basin).

Reliance Petrochemicals

Reliance is one of the major players in the petrochemical sector in India. It is the flagship company of the Reliance Group and is considered as the largest private sector company of the country. The Reliance Industries manufactures maximum polyester yarn and fibre in the world and also enjoys a high position across the globe for the promotion of major petrochemical products.

The Reliance Industries has earned a benchmark in the production of the petrochemical products from crude oil to natural gas exploration and production to other variants of petrochemicals.

Regarding the use of petrochemical product like polymers, the Reliance Industries is a major producer of product brands like Repol, Relene, Reclair, Reon, and Relpipe. The company produces Linear Alkyl Benzene under the name of Relab. The other brands of products of the Reliance Petrochemicals are also popular in the market.

Reliance is not only the largest producer of polyester fibre and yarn in the world but it is the fourth largest producer of Paraxylene, fifth largest producer of Purified Terepthalic Acid, and seventh largest producer of Polypropylene.

Reliance Life Sciences

Reliance Life Sciences (RLS) is a millennium initiative of the Reliance Group. The Group initially has invested $5 million in setting up facilities in cell biology in Mumbai. And the embryonic stem cell work began in April 2001.

The Reliance Industries Ltd will be investing about $25 million in cell biology research to focus on stem cells and tissue engineering. This covers embryonic stem cells, haematopoietic stem cells, skin cells, tissue engineering, genetics and molecular diagnostics. RLS' facility at Jamnagar primarily focuses on plant biotechnology projects where modern farming methods are being tried in arid areas. In addition to this, Jamnagar also has facilities for carrying out industrial biotechnology research by addressing the biopolymers, bio-fuels and bio-process development opportunities.

Besides stem cell research, RLS is developing business opportunities in the domains of medical biotechnology, plant biotechnology, industrial biotechnology, contract research and clinical trials.

RLS is in the process of setting up its Cord Blood Repository (CBR) and plans to grow the repository to around 30,000 units over the next two-three years. It has filed about nine patents in India and has been offering few products and services in both medical and plant biotechnology space. With a strong team of scientists and researchers numbering over 100, it already has products and services in medical biotech such as ReliCord, ImmunoRel, AlbuRel, and ReliSeal.

Reliance Industries Ltd has set 2009-10 as a threshold year to emerge as a global energy major. To achieve this, life sciences has been identified as its next major initiative.

Reliance Retails

Reliance is gearing up to revolutionize the retailing industry in India. Towards this end, Reliance is aggressively working on introducing a pan-India network of retail outlets in multiple formats.

A world class shopping environment, state of art technology, a seamless supply chain infrastructure, a host of unique value-added services and above all, unmatched customer experience, is what this initiative is all about.

The retail initiative of Reliance will be without a parallel in size and spread and make India proud. Ensuring better returns to Indian farmers and manufacturers and greater value for the Indian consumer, both in quality and quantity, will be an integral feature of this project. By creating value at all levels, we will actively endeavour to contribute to India's growth.

The project will boast of a seamless supply chain infrastructure, unprecedented even by world standards. Through multiple formats and a wide range of categories, Reliance is aiming to touch almost every Indian customer and supplier.

Reliance Logistics

Reliance Logistics offers a complete solution to export and import business by rendering range of services like Air Freight, Ocean Freight, and multimodal transport operation forwarding and door to door services.

Having worked with customers from different industries, trade and commerce, the company has acquired its reputation as the most efficient and professional forwarding company. By understating the global challenges in today's business, the company offers various kinds of optional services on shipping and transportation needs to the customers, enabling them to obtain reliable, cost effective, and time bound shipping solution.

Company experts have extensive knowledge on logistics and supply chain management and since they are equipped with clear understanding of 'Know how' in forwarding business. As a logistics partner, Reliance has always explored the needs of the customers and come up with best design to offer the cost effective and qualitative solutions to meet the shipping and logistics challenges.

Its dedicated resources are always standing by in order to provide the latest update on the shipment's status. From export-import documentation to trade management, its professionals have always been trustworthy business partners of the customers.

The company has vision of becoming the market leader in logistic business and developing the infrastructure to extend integrated logistics and supply chain management solutions.

Reliance Solar

The solar energy initiative of Reliance aims to bring solar energy systems and solutions primarily to remote and rural areas and bring about a transformation in the quality of life.

As part of this initiative, Reliance Solar is developing and offering a range of products, systems and solutions—from solar lanterns, home lighting systems, street lighting systems, water purification systems, refrigeration systems to solar air conditioners—all based on solar energy.

These products, systems and solutions are part of the downstream component of the solar value chain. Reliance Solar is concurrently working on developing the upstream and midstream components in an integrated manner- from polysilicon to ingots, wafers, cells and modules.

Reliance Industrial Infrastructure

The Company was incorporated in September 1988 as a Public Limited Company in the name of 'Chembur Patalganga Pipelines Limited'. The name of the Company was subsequently changed to 'CPPL Limited' in September 1992 and thereafter to its present name in March 1994.

The company commenced its commercial operation in March 1992. The company is mainly engaged in the business of setting up/operating Industrial Infrastructure. The company is also engaged in related activities involving leasing and providing services connected with computer software and data processing.

The company has set up a 200-millimetre dia twin pipeline system from the Refinery of Bharat Petroleum Corporation at Mahul, Mumbai, for transporting petroleum products like Naphtha and Kerosene to the Petrochemical Complex of Reliance Industries Limited at Patalganga.

The company has acquired and deployed various construction machineries on hire for use at various construction sites all over India.

The company has its operations in Mumbai and the Rasayani regions of Maharashtra, Surat and Jamnagar belts of Gujarat, also at other places in India.

Jamnagar Refinery

The Jamnagar Complex is the first manufacturing complex of its kind, having a fully integrated petroleum refinery, petrochemicals complex, captive power plants, and a captive port, with related infrastructure. It represents the largest single investment at a single site in India.

The refinery comprises more than 50 process units. Some of the processes being used by the refinery encompass crude oil distillation, catalytic cracking, catalytic reforming and delayed coking.

The refinery project required a total investment of Rs 9,700 crore ($207 million) which was a fraction of the total project cost of Rs 20,400 crore ($437 million).

Construction of the plant commenced in 1996 and had an initial construction period of 29-30 months. However, Reliance pushed contractors to work on a two shift-24hr basis so as to have the site finished within a 24-month period. After completion the refinery had a capacity to produce 15 million tonnes per year of refined crude.

❑

"Between my past, the present and the future, there is one common factor: Relationship and Trust. This is the foundation of our growth."

—*Dhirubhai Ambani*

Anil Ambani

Anil Ambani is one of the topmost entrepreneurs of Independent India. He is the Chairman of Anil Dhirubhai Ambani Group. Earlier, before the split in the Reliance Group, Anil Ambani held the post of Vice Chairman and Managing Director in Reliance Industries Limited (RIL).

Born on June 4, 1959, Anil Ambani did his Bachelors in Science from the University of Mumbai and Masters in Business Administration from the Wharton School at the University of Pennsylvania.

Anil Ambani joined Reliance, the company founded by his late father Dhirubhai Ambani, in 1983 as Co-Chief Executive

A great sports enthusiast

Officer and is credited with having pioneered many financial innovations in the Indian capital markets. He directed Reliance in its efforts to raise, since 1991, around US$2 billion from overseas financial markets; with a 100-year Yankee bond issue in January 1997 being the high point, after which people regarded him as a financial wizard. He along with his brother, Mukesh Ambani, has steered the Reliance Group to its current status as India's leading textiles, petroleum, petrochemicals, power, and telecom company.

Anil Dhirubhai Ambani serves as President of the Dhirubhai Ambani Institute of Information and Communications Technology. Mr. Ambani served as Managing Director of Reliance Infrastructure Ltd (formerly, Reliance Energy Ltd and BSES Ltd). from April 2003 to April 24, 2007.

Anil Ambani served as an Executive Officer of Reliance Telecom Ltd. He served as Managing Director and Vice-Chairman of Reliance Industries Ltd. from July 31, 2002 to June 2005. He served as Managing ... Director of Reliance Petroleum Ltd. from April 2003 to April 24, 2007. From June 2004 to March 25, 2006, Mr. Ambani served as an Independent Member of the Rajya Sabha, Upper House of India's Parliament.

Anil Ambani serves as Chairman of Reliance Power Limited. He has been Chairman of Reliance Capital Ltd. since June 19, 2005 and has been Non Executive Chairman of Reliance Infrastructure Ltd., since April 2007. He serves as Chairman of the Board of Reliance Communications Ltd. Mr. Ambani serves as Chairman and Director of Reliance - Anil Dhirubhai Ambani Group, Reliance Communications Infrastructures Ltd., Reliance Telecom Ltd., Reliance Communication Ventures Ltd.,

Reliance Capital Ventures Ltd., Reliance Energy Ventures Ltd., and Reliance Natural Resources Ltd.

He serves as non-executive Chairman of Reliance Infratel Limited. He served as Chairman of the Board of Reliance Infrastructure Ltd., from April 2003 to April 24, 2007. He served as Chairman and Director of FLAG Telecom Group Ltd. (owned by Reliance Infocomm) since July 2005. He served as Chairman of the Board of Reliance Infocomm Limited. He served as Vice Chairman of Indian Petrochemicals Corporation Limited until January 4, 2005.

Anil Ambani has been a Director of Reliance Infrastructure Ltd., since January 18, 2003. He has been a Non-Executive Director of Reliance Infratel Limited since June 18, 2007 and serves as its Member of Advisory Board. He has been a Director of Reliance Power Limited. since September 2007 and also serves as its Member of Advisory Board. He has been a Director of Reliance Communications Ltd. since February 7, 2006.

He serves as a Member of the Executive Board at Indian School of Business (ISB). Mr. Ambani serves as a Member of

Anil Ambani with his wife and son

Wharton Board of Overseers, the Wharton School, USA, Central Electricity Regulatory Commission, Chairman, the Board of Governors of the National Safety Council, the Board of Governors of Indian Institute of Management, Ahmedabad and the Board of Governors of Indian Institute of Technology, Kanpur. He served as a Director of Reliance Petroleum Ltd.

He was conferred 'the Chief Executive Officer of the Year 2004' in the Platts Global Energy Awards. He was rated as one of 'India's Most Admired Chief Executive Officers' for the sixth consecutive year in the Business Barons - TNS Mode opinion poll, 2004. He was conferred 'The Entrepreneur of the Decade Award' by the Bombay Management Association, October 2002.

He was also awarded the First Wharton Indian Alumni Award by the Wharton India Economic Forum (WIEF) in recognition of his contribution to the establishment of Reliance as a global leader in many of its business areas, December 2001.

·❑

"For those who dare to dream, there is a whole world to win!"

—Dhirubhai Ambani

Reliance ADA Group

Reliance Anil Dhirubhai Ambani Group came into existence when the business empire of the Reliance Group founded by Dhirubhai Ambani was split between his two sons, Mukesh and Anil. Mukesh, the elder brother, retained Reliance Industries Limited (RIL), the flagship company of the Reliance Group. The part of the empire that was inherited by the younger brother Anil was christened as Reliance Anil Dhirubhai Ambani Group.

Hence, one can say that the founder of Reliance ADAG was Dhirubhai Ambani. The interests of the Reliance Anil Dhirubhai Ambani span communications, financial services, generation, transmission and distribution of power, infrastructure and entertainment.

Reliance Communications

Reliance Communications is India's largest information and communications service provider with over 75 million subscribers. The company is the realisation of our founder's dream of bringing about a digital revolution that will provide every Indian with affordable means of communication and a ready access to information.

The flagship company of the Reliance – ADA Group, Reliance Communications began operations in 1999 and has over 75 million subscribers today. It offers a complete range of integrated telecom services. These include mobile and fixed line telephony, broadband, national and international long distance services, data services and a wide range of value added services and applications aimed at enhancing the productivity of enterprises and individuals.

Reliance Globalcom, a division of Reliance Communications, spearheads the Global Telecom operations of India's largest Integrated Telecom Service Provider. Reliance Globalcom brings together the synergies of Reliance Communications Global Business encompassing Enterprise Services, Capacity Sales, Managed Services and a highly successful bouquet of retail products & services comprising Global Voice, Internet Solutions and Value Added Services. The company serves over 1200 enterprises, 200 carriers and 1.5 million retail customers in 50 countries across 5 continents.

Reliance Health

In a country where healthcare is fast becoming a booming industry, Reliance Health is a focused healthcare services company enabling the provision of solution to Indians, at affordable prices. The company aims at providing integrated health services that will compete with the best in the world. It also plans to venture into diversified fields like Insurance Administration, Health care Delivery and Integrated Health, Health Informatics and Information Management and Consumer Health.

Reliance Health aims at revolutionising healthcare in India by enabling a healthcare environment that is both affordable and accessible through partnerships with government and private businesses.

Reliance Power

Reliance Power Limited is part of the Reliance Anil Dhirubhai Ambani Group and is established to develop,

Corporate Guru: Dhirubhai Ambani

construct and operate power projects domestically and internationally. The Company on its own and through subsidiaries is currently developing 13 medium and large sized power projects with a combined planned installed capacity of 28,200 MW, one of the largest portfolios of power generation assets under development in India.

Reliance Big Entertainment

Reliance Big Entertainment has evolved out of the group's vision of meeting young India's aspirations and assuming a leadership position in communications, media and entertainment. Reliance Big Entertainment is geared to create a significant presence in businesses across various vectors of content, internet, broadcast and retail services and platforms for distribution. The company strives to create converged services and platforms for masses to access innovative, cutting-edge content. Key content initiatives include production and strategic collaboration in areas such as gaming, movies, animation, music, broadcast, DTH and user-generated content, amongst others.

Reliance Infrastructure

Reliance Infrastructure Ltd is not only India's largest private sector enterprise in power utility but also the largest private sector player in many other infrastructure sectors of India. In the power sector it involved in generation, transmission, distribution and trading of electricity and constructing power plants as EPC partners. In the infrastructure concern, the company is focused on roads, urban infrastructure which includes MRTS, Sealink and Airports, Specialty Real Estate which includes business districts, trade towers, convention centre and SEZ which includes IT & ITES SEZ and non IT SEZ as well as free trade zones.

Reliance Capital

Reliance Capital is one of India's leading and fastest growing private sector financial services companies, and ranks among the top 3 private sector financial services and banking companies, in terms of net worth.

Reliance Capital has interests in asset management and mutual funds, life and general insurance, private equity investments, stock broking and other activities in financial services.

Reliance BPO

Reliance BPO is a premium BPO & KPO service provider offering cutting edge solutions to global Communications, BFSI, Utility and Entertainment industries.

Mudra Communications

As a part of Reliance ADA Group Ltd., Mudra rose to become the third largest agency in the country in a short span of 9 years. Today, the Mudra Group, with more than 125 clients nationwide with three creative agencies, eight full service offices, seven specialised business units and an integrated media offering, has a portfolio of some of India's biggest brand

NIS Sparta

NIS Sparta is a division of Mudra Communications Pvt. Ltd., a Reliance ADA group organisation. NIS Sparta is Asia's leading training, education and learning solutions provider.

❑

"I dream India of becoming a great economic superpower."
　　　　　　　　　　　—*Dhirubhai Ambani*

Tête-â-Tête with Anil Ambani

Reliance Industries has denied charges that the group had thrived on the pre-reform 'licence raj' of the 1970s and 1980s to become the country's largest private entity, and attributed the growth to the vision of group's patriarch Dhirubhai Ambani.

"The licence raj prevailed for everybody, not only for us. You can get an industry licence to set up a plant, but that doesn't raise your financing, it doesn't raise your technology, it doesn't produce your quality, it doesn't market your products, it doesn't help you raise money from the capital markets. You don't suddenly get 3-4 million shareholders into the company."

"India went for reforms in 1991. The growth for Reliance has been the highest in the last ten years than it was in permit raj. I don't see any harm in building relationships with people whether it's my customer or my vendor, whether it is my shareholder, or somebody in a position of power whom we need to convince about our case.

Nobody can say that we have run away with anybody's money. Though I can give you a list of Indians who've taken their companies bankrupt," said Ambani.

Ambani spoke about various aspects of his life, his education and his business. Excerpts:

On what life has taught him

"I think I'd like to put it differently, and look at what have been the key messages thrown at us over the last two or three decades that I've been in corporate life. And those have certainly been my father's core values that were ingrained in us: being down to earth, being humble, and being very simple. That's how he is even today and I think that's a big message for us."

On childhood memories

Many years ago, our family lived in the backstreets of Mumbai, in a *chawl* at Kabootarkhana, which was a co-operative housing society, where over six hundred families lived together. Everyone had a one-bedroom accommodation. People find it shocking that neither I nor Mukesh drink or smoke, are vegetarian, are god fearing, and don't gamble.

These are not values that are passed on by any sort of action, but more a part of one's upbringing. Praying to god, respecting other individuals...I think it's been really put together by my mother. My father was very, very busy.

On his parents

My mother is a very simple down-to-earth person. My grandfather, was a postman. He rose to become the in-charge of a post-office in Jamnagar in Gujarat. So she comes from that background.

Her marriage to my father was, obviously, an arranged one. My paternal grandfather was a schoolteacher. Soon after my parents got married, they went to Aden in Yemen. That's where he started working as a gas station attendant (a petrol pump attendant in Indian parlance), and typically he went there to raise capital, conserve capital and come back.

My mother really supported my father through those tough times. I don't think I recall — during my entire school or college career—my father spending time with me, sitting with my homework or my tuitions or anything of this sort.

It was left to my mother, who was just a high-school graduate, to be on our case. However, not knowing the content she couldn't really add value to what we really wanted to do.

My father looked at it very simply, saying "I think we are going to give you the best upbringing to help create the best values for you. I believe you have the brains so you should study hard. You don't have the financial problems that I had when I wanted to study. Well, you don't have any monetary problems, so go and try to look for the best school, college, university that you can go to."

Time and again, I've asked him what he misses most, and he always said that it has been a good education. He wanted to study, but he didn't have the resources. Fortunately, in our case, we had no such problem.

I was 10-years-old when we moved out of the *chawl*. I have clear memories of living there. It had one bedroom; we were seven members in the family, including my grandmother. There was a common bathroom and toilet for a hundred families together in the *chawl*.

It was on the fourth floor, that's about a flight of 50-60 steps. We stayed at Kabootarkhana, Bhuleshwar; I think it was called Jaihind Estate.

On values

We moved to Usha Kiran later. But nothing came very easy. We had no lack of monetary resources, but we were given sort of goal-oriented finances. This was very important; my father would ask us to do something to earn.

For example, if we played a match or went hiking or trekking or walking or whatever else…. At the end of the trek, he would give us a choice of two things: we could have one drink and one snack, or two snacks and no drink. The budget was five bucks, and it didn't change for a long time.

I recall it was the summer of early 1970s and he said to us, "Look this is the mango season, I know you guys are very fond of mangoes, but the only ways you can get a full box of mangoes is if you travel by the lower deck on the Mumbai to Goa steamer. And, you know, our incentive was the mangoes, not the trip to Goa!

He could afford to send us by air, yes. But he wanted us to go through that "lower deck experience", where there was no reservation and everybody was puking. He just wanted us to go through that event because he believed that there is no way we could ever buy that sort of experience.

On his education

In 1981, I went to the Wharton School at the University of Pennsylvania to do my masters in Business Administration. That was the first time I was leaving home alone. Typical of all mothers, mine was apprehensive. She told my father, "He is going to a faraway place, he has never lived alone, he is a vegetarian... He will die of starvation, so why don't we send somebody along with him..."

My father said, "Absolutely not. He is going to stay on the campus for the next 18 to 24 months. That experience is going to be invaluable. It cannot be measured in terms of money; it is going to be infinite in terms of value."

That's where I learnt how to cook, clean up, ash and iron my clothes, clean my toilet, etc. That was a huge confidence-building exercise.

On learning the ropes

When I came back, I still recall it was the 2nd of December 1982, 3 o'clock when I finished my last exam at Wharton. I took the 8 o'clock flight from New York, which is three hours' drive from Philadelphia and landed in Mumbai on the night of December 3.

On 4th of December, I met him and said dad I've graduated, I've got my masters. I've done it in 14 months, instead of 24 months! So its time for a break; you know take two-three weeks off and 'chill out'. He said, "Absolutely not. You are going this evening to Ahmedabad and that's where you will stay for the next few years and look after our textile business."

So I asked, "Should *I* not get a break?" He said, "There will be enough time in the future for you to enjoy life, this is the time for you to work." And that was it, there was no further argument, there was no debate and I took the evening flight and I stayed for the next five-six years in Ahmedabad, five days a week at our textile plant.

My father thought that working from the shop floor, all the way to the top, was the right way to do it. He left me with one very simple message when I left. He said, "Look, you have the choice. You have the ability either to command respect or to demand respect. Choice is yours. People will respect you when you are in the commanding mode, because of what you are. If you are in the demanding mode, then they won't respect you and bitch about you as soon as you turn your back to them."

On life after his father's stroke

My father had a stroke in 1986. Both Mukesh and I were in mid twenties then. That was the real period of exposure for us; challenges, growth, and "the era of tempering steel" - as my father fondly refers it — because that's the time we were exposed to every possible adversity that anybody can think of. And we had to battle through all of that and I think those years of learning are very, very precious.

Getting an MBA clearly didn't teach me how to manage the environment in India after I came back. My father's description of an MBA in Gujarati is *"Mane badhu aawe chhe* (I know everything). And that is how all MBA, behave once they graduate. The feeling is "Hey! You guys don't know anything. I am 22-years-old and I know everything." I think during that stage — from 1986 to 1989-90 — we had a large number of factions working against us in number of ways.

I still recall that after the first few weeks when my father was recovering, I asked him what he thought about the way things were building up. He said, "That's part of life. It's the Indian crab theory, so don't worry about it." He always refers to all the people who are so-called adversaries as "the well-wishers of Reliance." Always, even today.

The task was clearly challenging. Today, one crore (10 million) means nothing much in rupee terms, but I do recall that I went on a number of occasions where a particular lender wanted his one crore back though it was not due. I must have gone and met him 16 times, I had to say, "Please don't take this one crore away." But they said, "No." I said, "Fine, I respect your instructions and we'll honour whatever we'll have to honour."

In the history of Reliance, we've never, ever defaulted, we've never even delayed repayments, and that is the trust and confidence and track record we enjoy today. That is clearly a value my father created.

There was a phase when many people said that it was over, that we might survive as a company, but the era of growth was over. They said even if my father resumed work after his stroke, he would never be back to his old self, and both of us (Mukesh and I) were just kids. But, both of us looked it as a great opportunity.

Whenever people tried to push us down, Mukesh — being an engineer — reminded us of Newton's third law: *every action has an equal and opposite reaction;* so the more the people pushed us down the more we sprang back and said we are going to prove everybody wrong and I think that's what we have done.

There was great determination, there was a great deal of commitment, and I would say there was an ultimate belief in God. We are believers in fate, destiny and *karma.* At the same time, you have to help yourself. You just can't be sitting on your chair and believe that Vir Sanghvi is going to interview you. You've got to show up at the studio and be in front of him....

On the major business shift of Reliance

I think it goes back to my father's vision. He had a vision when he was a petrol-pump attendant in Aden and later grew up to be a marketing manager. He also worked on a small refinery in Aden and dreamt that some day he would get into the energy and oil business.

So as we looked at the growth of Reliance, we charted the course for vertical backward integration. The only reason to start that way was we had no access to capital. This was a first-generation enterprise.

So we started with textiles, which was the least capital-intensive. Then we went back to manufacture of polyester and then all the way upstream to oil and gas exploration, refining, marketing of petroleum, petrochemicals, plastics, the entire energy chain... That's how we really did it.

Till 1977, early 1978, Reliance Textile Industries was a private limited company... we then went public and are a largely publicly held company now.

On his sons

I've two sons, Anshul and Anmol. They are 11 and 6. My father still insists they travel second-class in the local trains, he insists we send them to school camps where a hundred children live in a dorm, and don't have a bath for three days... so they are going through that sort of thing.

They follow values: they don't see me eating meat — nothing religious about it, just a personal choice — so they follow that, they don't see me smoking, so they follow that too.

On his routine and fitness

I get up at 5:30 every day to go for jogging. I do a variety of things. I run about half a marathon a week... I am learning how to play polo. I swim, I do all sorts of funny things.

Maybe that keeps me going and that's my intoxication, my high, my level of satisfaction. That comes through my physical performance or my achievement.

I think it was a couple of years ago when I was at an investors' meeting in New York and one of the investors after the presentation was over said, "Well, Mr Ambani, the company looks in great shape and we have great confidence in its future. But have you looked at yourself recently in the mirror?" And I said well that's a personal question, can we discuss it separately and he said, "No. I have the guts to ask this question in front of everybody, so I need the answer now." I said, "No I've not looked at myself recently in the mirror." Well, he said, "If you are not in a good shape, I don't think your company can be in good shape."

I came back after that presentation looked at myself at the mirror; I was a hundred and three kilos in weight and I said, "I look awful."

So a couple of years ago I started a programme, which is not a typical diet programme… just a change in lifestyle programme. Happily, I shed 35 kilos and I've changed my complete lifestyle to whatever I think is going to sustain me and I am doing pretty well.

I am lower in my weight than when I was in 1981 and possibly fitter than before. I just have to improve my physical performance a bit more and maybe one of these days I'll officially run a marathon. I've run that couple of times in Mumbai, but not in a competitive environment.

(Reliance group Vice-Chairman Anil Ambani, in an interview conducted by Vir Sanghvi for Star Talk)

❏

"If you work with determination and with perfection, success will follow."

—*Dhirubhai Ambani*

PERSONAL DETAILS
IN NUTSHELL

Timeline Dhirubhai

- **Name:** Dhirajlal Hirachand Ambani
- **Status:** Founder and Chairman of Reliance Group
- **Date of birth:** December 28, 1932
- **Place of Birth:** Chorwad village in Saurashtra, Gujarat
- **Father's name:** Hirachand Govardhandas Ambani
- **Mother's name:** Jamunaben Hirachand Ambani
- **Marital Status:** Married to Kokilaben. Four children — sons Mukesh and Anil, daughters Dipti Salgaonkar, living in Goa, and Nina Kothari, living in Chennai.
- **Business Address:** Maker Chambers IV, 222, Nariman Point, Mumbai 400 021
- **Names of major companies:** Reliance Industries Ltd, Reliance Petroleum Ltd Directorships, Chairmanships: Reliance Industries Ltd, Reliance Petroleum Ltd.
- **Career:** At the age of 17, Dhirubhai went to Aden (now in Yemen) and worked for '*A Besse and Co Ltd,*' the sole distributor of Shell products.

  Returned to Mumbai in 1958 and started his first company— Reliance Commercial Corp, a commodity trading and exports house.

  Started textile mill in Naroda in Ahmedabad in 1966.

  In 1975, a technical team of the World Bank certified that the Reliance textile plant was 'excellent' according to developed country standards.

  The company went public in 1997.

The group is credited with a number of financial innovations in the Indian capital market.

Today the group has the largest family of shareholders in the world.

With an investment of Rs 360 billion in petroleum refining, petrochemicals, power generation, telecommunication services and a port terminal in a three-year time frame, the late Dhirubhai Ambani had steered the Group to its current status as India's leading textiles-petrochemicals-telecommunications player.

Reliance Group is India's largest business house with total revenues of over Rs 600 billion, cash flow of Rs 70 billion, net profit of Rs 45 billion and exports of Rs 93.70 billion.

With total assets of Rs 550 billion, the group's activities span petrochemicals, synthetic fibres, fibre intermediaries, textiles, oil and gas, financial services, refining and marketing, power, insurance, telecom and infocom initiatives.

Reliance emerged as India's most admired business house in a Taylor Nelson Sofres-Mode (TSN-Mode) survey for 2001 conducted by *Business Barons* magazine.

Achievements

- Conferred the lifetime achievement award by India HRD Congress in February 2002. Conferred *The Economic Times* award for corporate excellence for lifetime achievement in August 2001. Thrice rated as 'India's Most Admired CEO' in the Business Barons-Taylor Nelson Sofres-Mode survey in June 2001, 2000 and 1999.

- Felicitated by the *Brihanmumbai Municipal Corporation*, the biggest civic body of the country, with a citation and address followed by civic reception in December 2002.

- Conferred the 'Man of the Century' award by Chemtech Foundation and chemical engineering world in recognition of his outstanding contribution to the growth and development of the chemical industry in India, in November 2000.

- Conferred the 'Indian Entrepreneur of the 20th century' award by FICCI for his meticulous scripting of one of the most remarkable stories of business endeavours, in March 2000.
- Thrice nominated as one of the 'Power 50-The Most Powerful People in Asia' by *Asia Week* magazine in 2000, 1998 and 1996 respectively.
- Voted as the 'Most Admired Indian of the Millennium' in the field of business and economics' in 'Legends- a celebration of Excellence' poll audited by Ernst and Young for Zee network in January 2000.
- Voted as 'Creator of Wealth of the Century' in 'The Times of India' poll in January 2000.
- Chosen as one of three 'makers of equity' by 'India Today' in their special millennium issue entitled '100 people who shaped India in the 20th Century' in January 2000.
- Chosen by the Indian Merchants Chamber as 'an outstanding visionary of the 20th century' for his achievements and contribution to the development of industry and capital markets in India, in December 1999.
- Voted as 'Indian Businessman of the Century' in *Business Barons* Global Multimedia poll December 1999.
- Amongst the 'Power 50- India's 50 most powerful decision maker in politics, business and finance' in *Business Barons* in August 1999.
- Declared 'Most admired Indian business leader' by *The Times of India*, indiatimes.com poll in July 1999.
- The only Indian industrialist in the 'Business Hall of Fame' in *Asia Week* in October 1998.
- Awarded the Dean's medal by the Wharton School, University of Pennslyvania, for setting an outstanding example of leadership, in June 1998.

- Chosen as 'Star of Asia' by *Business Week*, USA in June 1998.
- *Business Barons* placed Ambani on its list of India's 25 most influential business and financial leaders, in June 1998.
- Awarded the Companion Membership of Textile Institute, UK, a membership which is limited to 50 living members, who have substantially advanced the general interests of industries based in fibres, in 1994.
- Chosen 'Businessman of the year 1993' by *Business India*, in January 1994.

❑

"Don't give up, courage is my conviction."

—Dhirubhai Ambani

Institutions in Memory of Dhirubhai

Many institutions of international standards have been setup in the memory of Late Dhirubhai Ambani. We provide some useful information about few prominent institutions for our readers, especially for the young ones.

Dhirubhai Ambani Knowledge City

Concurrent with the launch of Reliance Infocom Ltd, the new-age initiative at the convergence of information technology and communications, the Reliance group had unveiled a new campus—the Dhirubhai Ambani Knowledge City (DAKC). This is the largest new economy campus in India.

A brainchild of Nita Ambani, the president of the Dhirubhai Ambani Foundation, DAKC is a world-class campus that showcases the spirit of the knowledge age in its layout, architecture and character.

Set amidst a picturesque 140-acre plot in Navi Mumbai, DAKC is the heart of Reliance Infocom. DAKC houses the national headquarters, Internet data centres, call centres, applications development laboratories and the national network operations centre of Reliance Infocom.

With 2.2-million sq ft of office space spread

over 14 buildings, DAKC has a capacity to house 10,000 people. To address needs of this magnitude, DAKC is fully equipped with several food courts, all utilities, ATM machines and business centres.

The architectural style adopted in DAKC is functional and elegant with extensive use of glass and granite for exteriors of the buildings, interspersed with extensive landscaping to provide visual relief. Signage, reflecting the blue and green colours of Reliance Infocomm, complements the visual identity of the campus.

Reliance Infocom has a very young employee profile with an average age of 32 years. This aspect lends character and charm to DAKC, and resonate the faith that Dhirubhai Ambani had in India's youth.

The highlight as well as the nerve centre of DAKC is a spectacular 110,000-sq ft National Network Operations Centre (NNOC). From here the entire network of Reliance Infocom, covering 60,000 kilometres of optic fibre that connects 90 per cent of India's population and reaching 600 towns and cities, is monitored and controlled.

The concept of one control centre for an entire network is unique and is unprecedented in the world. Unlike most other network operations centres around the world, which are designed to support a specific product, service or geography, the NNOC of Reliance Infocom is unique in the sense that it controls range of products, services and geographies.

The main control room with a seating capacity for 200 has two large video walls, each 100-feet long and with 80 screens each. A hanging bridge running across the control room is part of the visitors' experience and an integral part of NNOC.

A picturesque lake on campus reflects the serenity of a temple on one side and the activity of the national headquarters building on the opposite side. In a sense, it contrasts the tradition with the modern.

DAKC is a homage as well as a reflection of the vision, enterprise and creativity of Dhirubhai Ambani, one of the greatest sons that India has ever produced.

Address: A campus/technology park located on the Thane-Belapur Road, Koparkhairane in Navi Mumbai.

Dhirubhai Ambani IICT

The Dhirubhai Ambani Institute of Information and Communication Technology or DA-IICT is located at Gandhi Nagar, Gujarat. Gujarat has seen many waves of educational innovation and this technological institute stands testament to the fourth wave. Dhirubhai Ambani Institute of Information and Communication Technology (DAIICT) Gandhinagar in Gujarat, which was established in the year 2001, is a non affiliating University.

The Gujarat legislature awarded the institute the status of a University and in 2004, the University was admitted in the list of the University Grants Commission. It does not receive any aid or other financial assistance from the State or the Central Government.

Address: Dhirubhai Ambani IICT, Near Indroda Circle, Gandhinagar - 382 007, Gujarat

❑

"You do not require an invitation to make profits."

—Dhirubhai Ambani

Vignettes from an Action-Packed Life

- In Aden, Dhirubhai Ambani worked at the Shell products division of A Besse & Co. He quickly made an impression on his colleagues by taking almost impossible bets. Once he bet that while helping bunker a ship in the harbour he could dive and swim to shore. The prize for winning the bet was an ice-cream party. Dhirubhai won the bet, even though it meant swimming through shark-infested waters.

- Dhirubhai Ambani was not one to let an opportunity slip by. One story - which may be apocryphal - runs as follows. During the 1950s the Yemeni administration discovered that the main unit of its currency, the rial, was disappearing from the market. The administration traced the shortage to Aden, a port in Yemen and found to its surprise that a young Indian in his twenties had placed an unlimited buy order for rials. The rial was a solid silver coin and what this young man did was to simply buy rials, melt them into silver ingots and sold them to bullion dealers in London. This was a profitable venture as the silver in the rial was valued higher by bullion dealers in London. The name of the young man? Dhirubhai Ambani.

  Later, Ambani is believed to have told an interviewer: "The margins were small but it was money for jam. After three months, it was stopped. But I made a few lakh of rupees. I don't believe in not taking opportunities."

- Dhirubhai was known for his practical jokes. Once he was invited by a friend to dine at his house. The friend's wife offered some mango juice and insisted on refilling Dhirubhai's glass. So he decided to play a prank. He kept asking for more mango juice, till the hosts ran out of mangoes and the servant was sent out to buy some more from the market.

In 1968, Dhirubhai moved out of the *chawl* in Mumbai where he lived, to a more comfortable flat on Altamount Road, in Mumbai's first high-rise residential tower. Dhirubhai had a penchant for driving fast cars. He first owned a modest Fiat and later acquired a Mercedes-Benz. In the seventies, he got a white Cadillac for himself.

On his return from Aden, Dhirubhai set up a trading business in 1957 in partnership with Chambaklal Damani, his second cousin who had also been in Aden around the same time. The name of their business: Reliance Commercial Corp. Their first office was a 350 sq ft room on Narsinathan Street in the crowded Masjid Bunder area of Mumbai. The room had a telephone, one table and three chairs. If both the partners and the first two recruits were present in the office, one of them had no place to sit.

❏

"I consider myself a pathfinder. I have been excavating the jungle and making the road for others to walk. I like to be the first in everything I do."

–Dhirubhai Ambani

Factfile of
Dhirubhai Ambani

- **28-12-1932**—Born to a Modh Bania family as the second son and fourth child of a teacher father.
- **1949-1958**—Went to Aden at the age of 17 after the death of his father discontinuing his studies. Worked as gas station attendant for A. Bessy & Co. a dealer of Burma Shell products. Rose to the post of General Marketing Manager. Became the father of elder son Mukesh on 19-4-1957.
- **1958-1965**—Returned to India. Set up Reliance Trading Company in Mumbai. Exported textiles and spices. Initially invested Rs. 15000 only.
- **1966**—As a first industrial venture founded Textile Mill at Naroda (Ahmedabad) and started work with 70 workers.
- **1975**—World Bank technical team visited Naroda Mill and certified it as a class enterprise of International standards.
- **1977**—Launched first Public Issue of Reliance Company starting Financial Equity culture in India. It proved a roaring success.
- **1978**—Reliance introduces its textile brand product 'Vimal' with much fanfare and unprecedented publicity. The Vimal Brand catches the imagination of the people and creates popularity records.
- **1979**—Came out with another Public Issue for starting a new 'Worsted Textile Mill'. The issue was subscribed in no time. The small investors again put faith in him.

- **1980**—A public Issue launched again for modernisation of Textile Mill. Again over subscribed.

- **1980**—A new 110 crore project was announced to use the capital raised for Fibres accessory units in Patalganga project.

- **1980-1982**—Dhirubhai's detractors and rivals remained active. Many conspiracies against him and his companies were hatched. The Bear share brokers tried to pull down Reliance share prices through a short-selling game plan. Dhirubhai got his shares bought enblock by friendly brokers to prevent the crash. He succeeded.

- **1983**—Dhirubhai was accused of buying his own shares through bogus companies in 'Isle of Man'. A probe was held but he was found innocent. There was nothing to pin on him.

- **1985**—Rasikbhai Meswani, his brother-in-law and a capable executive of Reliance passed away. The loss was irreparable. Corporate war with Nusli Wadia of Bombay Dyeing began. Some decisions of the then finance minister, V.P. Singh also caused huge losses to his industrial house.

- **1986**—Healthwise the year was traumatic for Dhirubhai Ambani. He was struck with a paralytic attack and had been taken to New York for treament. In his absence some projects slowed down or faced other hurdles. The profits of Reliance dipped down.

- **1987**—His sons took over most of his responsibilities. It was a big relief for Dhirubhbai and a cause for pride and satisfaction. The two brothers successfully completed and commissioned Polyster Staple Fibre and Purified Teupltholic Acid units at Patalganga project.

- **1988**—That year Dhirubhai's great ambition was fulfilled. His plants started production of Fibre intermediate and chemicals. He gained management control over public undertaking Larsen & Tubro. It was a hugely prestigious posting as Chairman.

- Public Issue of Reliance Petrochemicals was launched for subscription. A record 2 million small investors applied.
- **1989**—Patalganga Complex suffered damages due to heavy floods.
- **1990**—In changed political scenario anticipating troubles he resigned from the chairmanship of 'Larsen & Tubro.'
- **1991**—Dhirubhai succeeded in realising his one other major dream of Rs. 9000 crore Hajira Project commissioned its first plant to the envy of his rivals and dismay of detractors.
- **1992**—Public issue to raise a capital of Rs. 325 crores for Reliance Polypropelence Ltd. and Reliance Polyethelene Ltd. was lauched. In this very year Reliance Group became first business and industrial house of India that started earning money from abroad through GDR.
- **1993**—Reliance entered distribution business as supplier of PVC and plastics.
- **1994**—The output capacity of Hajira Petrochemicals Complex was reviewed and increased to 6 million metric tons a year. Work on it was started at once without any delay.
- **1995**—The scandal of Reliance bogus shares broke out and inquiry was held.
- **1996**—SSP and Moodies included Reliance Group in 'World Class Industrial Houses' list. It was the first honour for an Indian private sector company.
- **1997**—Reliance Industries commissions world's biggest 'Multifeed Petrochemicals Cracker' at its Hajira facility. Reliance became Asia's first company. The group also started Cellular Services from this year in the country.
- **1998**—The worth of assets of Reliance Group of Industries crossed Rs. 35,000 crores and the earning figures rose above Rs. 14,000 crores.
- **1999**—World's largest oil refinery was commissioned in the

form of Jamnagar Refinery Complex. It was the proud moment for Dhirubhai Ambani and the entire nation.

- **2000**—Reliance announced three ambitious new ventures in communications field namely Reliance Infocom, Reliance Telecom and Reliance Communications. Reliance projects made improvements. Worth of its assets crossed Rs. 50,000 crores mark and output figures went above Rs. 20,000 crores.
- **2001**—'Reliance Life Science' chapter was started.
- **2002**—RPL was merged into RIL, in the same year Reliance Group acquired IPCL, a public sector undertaking.
- **July 6, 2002**—India lost its brilliant entrepreneur, Dhirubhai Ambani. He breathed his last in Breach Candy Hospital of Mumbai. A dream came to an end. But his dream projects remain to remind us of his economic and industrial vision.

❑

"We cannot change our rulers, but we can change the way they rule us."

—Dhirubhai Ambani